TABLE OF CONTENTS

Introduction/Overview

Land Development: Implication and Application

* *Background Checks and Vetting*
* *Developers: Toward a definition*
* *Land use Law: The reality of it all*

Case Study: Urban Development Management

* *Waterfront Development in Seaport Cities*
* *Urban Development Projects*
* *Urban Icons and Catalyst Effects*
* *Government Types and Impact on race and Urban Development*

Mayors, Developers and Economic Concerns: Introduction

Mayors, Developers and the Political Economics of the City

* *New York Mayors Michael Bloomberg/Bill de Blasio and the Developers*
* *Los Angeles Mayor Rick Caruso and the Developers*

  ✓ Los Angeles Ethics Commission and the Developers

* *Cincinnati Mayor's Race and the Developers*
* Lexington, Kentucky Mayor's Race and the Developers
* Palo Alto, California Mayor's Re-Election and the Developers
* Fort Myers, Florida, Mayor's Campaign Chest and the Developers

INTRODUCTION/OVERVIEW

The fact is, planners and developers work together to construct the configuration and housing (and racial) patterns of cities. The latter group, developers, also uses its financial power to dictate who will lead a particular city and serve as mayor. That is the thrust of this book: the "sociopolitical realities" of developers and how they team up with city administrations to constrict, control and encroach upon inner city areas and minority populations. This book is therefore historical, sociological, anthropological, and politico-economic.

As an African-American urbanologist I see a kind of "trilogy of treachery" when it comes to the lily-whiteness and on-going land abuse and thievery that has taken place in the name of "urban planning." You have the planners, the mayors of various cities and then come the developers with their buddies the "contractors." In the beginning the trilogy was comprised somewhat differently, a point I wish to touch upon it in an introduction before moving on to expose, castigate and critically analyze the "developers" of today.

White nationalism ruled supreme in the United States and, as such, it was inevitable that it would trickle down to the people who were planning the cities. This was not just a national reality: it was international. Take note of the following:

> At America's first urban planning conference, held in New York in 1898, *a British planner* asked whether he and his colleagues were striving for beautiful people or beautiful cities. Is urban planning about physical design, he wondered, or about making things easier for the people who live in our urban spaces? It was an essential question for the field, which really wasn't born until the early 20th century (Erikson, 2012 – emphasis added).

I have been in higher education as a student, counselor and teacher since 1973. I have debated and otherwise interacted with the best minds that the white race has to produce. And no matter what their background or pedigree, I have found one constant: when they come across new information or insights, and if those insights are not in the best interests of their race – no matter how well documented – they will go into escapist denial mode and retreat from the conversation. And they will engage in intellectual denial.

I have also found this tendency in their writings. A key component of history is that once "freed," a black exodus took place with African-Americans moving to the north mistakenly believing there was greater opportunity. But what they found is that the slave masters whip and the sharecropper's abuses of their harvests was replaced with the planner, the developer and the land use manipulator.

The desired effect – black relocation and exodus – had been achieved. This information is important not only to understand why an interest in the "cities" became significant, but so that you the reader can see the link that urban planning and race have conjointly played in the shaping of this country. Just as Omaha whites now try to take control of the "neighborhood movement" and launch it into a national organizational structure, they usually omit the role that the black presence played in giving form and function to neighborhood development, long before it was 'in vogue'.

The history of urban planning continues:

> Before then, there were three types of people thinking about how a city should look and function — architects, public health officials, and social workers. Each group approached the question of city building very differently (Erikson, 2012).

Let's use 1898 as the starting point. Today, in 2016, the three types of people who continue to dominate and direct the area of urban planning, complete with profit motive, are the architects, public health officials and the social workers. To that group you might want to add land developers, who work hand-in-hand with the architects to design where the people should live and who work with city planners to use zoning principles to ensure that those areas will remain residentially segregated.

Following is the "pie-in-the-sky" roles and goals of the three groups mentioned earlier and what their alleged intentions were for the city. First, the architects:

> The architects were focused on the city as a built environment, implementing ideas like L'Enfant's grand vision for Washington, D.C., and the New York City grid (set out by the Commissioner's Plan of 1811) … (Erikson, 2012).

What was just described was the glitz and glamour side of urban planning. That is the side where the skyscrapers, and then much later the skywalks and such are erected to give shape to the city's skyline. But these same architects are the ones who designed the kind of "public housing" that low-income people and minorities would be relegated to. They constructed those death traps that came to be known as "high-rise apartments." Eventually torn down after hundreds of murders and accidental deaths, some of those "architectural high rises for the poor" (as I call them) included Chicago's Cabrini Green or Robert Taylor Homes.

Segregation by class and race is a priority and precondition of these architects and the developers who work with them. They know that the people who can afford to live in certain buildings or tour and look at certain structures do not want to interact with (or have to look at) people who are "different." Architects are no more than the context to which they owe their existence; so they are as racist in their renderings and blueprints as the rest of the society is in its values and culture.

Then come the public health professionals:

> The public health professionals, on the other hand, were consumed with infrastructure. They knew there was a connection between certain diseases and social conditions, even if they didn't know precisely what it was. Planning how a water system would work, or where waste should go, or how to get garbage out of a city, was the most effective way to stop diseases from spreading (see, for example, John Snow, who figured out in the 1850s that a single water pump on Broad Street in London had infected hundreds of people with cholera). (Erikson, 2012).

Don't get it twisted: the "health professionals" were just as biased as the social workers and the architects. In fact, they were even more diabolical in their on-going quest to use people of color as guinea pigs. It was the health professional who paved the way for the Tuskegee Experiment where black men were infected and never told that they had the disease. It was the health professional who was right there with human experimentation on low-income and minority prisoners. And the list goes on and on. Their interest in the city was just as greed-and-grab oriented as any other people who were looking for ways to keep black people at bay while at the same time using them to generate research money and create jobs.

Continuing:

> And lastly the social workers wanted to use the city to improve
> the lives of the people living there. They wanted cleaner
> tenements, spaces for immigrant children to play, and more light
> and fresh air for residents (Erikson, 2012). (Erikson, 2012).

Such bullshit. Those social workers saw dollar signs. They knew that increased work hours, new "programs and services" and so on, all aimed at "helping the needy" would enrich their (social worker) coffers. Why would they truly give a damn about the people living in the city when they looked down on those people from the get-go?

All this paved the way for white "progress." In other words,

> These thinkers were brought together by the pressure cooker that
> was the Industrial Revolution. "At that moment, we began to look
> for technological ways to expand the city," says Elliott Sclar, a
> professor of urban planning at Columbia University. "All of a
> sudden here's a pressure to comprehensively plan. You can't just
> put a privy wherever you want." (Erikson, 2012).

Expanding the city doesn't mean that social workers wanted to expand their hours or their duties! With expansion of the city came the need for MORE pay and more worker's related rights. The city meant that the rules had to be re-written, more policies put in place to protect the rights and interests of owners and to subjugate the "owned." As is the case with those who live in public housing, the 4th Amendment rights of poor people are usually pushed to the side: the right to privacy and protection against illegal search and seizure don't mean anything when you are minority and/or low income and as such, you have become a target of the police power!

As modes of transportation changed, the need for better streets came about, cities began to get larger and the need for "planning" and "developing" for the towns that were growing into cities was badly needed:

> At that conference, and in the years that followed, any one of
> these early urban planning strains could have taken over as the
> intellectual giant in the field. Though the social workers and the
> public health officials continued to play a role, urban planning's
> intellectual history ended up grounded in architecture (Erikson,
> 2012).

I don't fully agree. When you are talking about being "grounded in architecture," you have to also consider the associated variables such as land acquisition, lot size, zoning codes and the like. Architects are leeches: they do the designing but all that has to fall in line with what the power structure dictates. The developers USE the architects to make physical and visible the vision that white folks have for a particular parcel of land or for a city. The social workers are used only to appease and placate the masses of people. In a word, urban planning's intellectual history is grounded in GREED; architecture is a reflection of that greed.

It is the developer who is key to the confusion and segregated state of the cities today. Greed and profit are the motivating factors. And it is the mayor or the city leader who is seeking out a "legacy project" or two to make sure that once he's gone his name will live on forever. Assisted by various city administrations (I name as many as space would allow), these developers and other wealthy shot-callers are financing political campaigns, shifting the political focus of city planners and in all that, rarely residing in the areas of the city that they are intentionally manipulating.

This book looks at eighteen (18) cities and towns, areas that represent populations from the mega-large (New York, Los Angeles, Pittsburgh) to the ultra small (Palm Springs, Hallendale Beach, Lexington, Kentucky) and focus on the relationship between the mayors of those cities and the developers and what the relationships are like. I believe this book will be a necessary and sufficient starting point for understand how real "land use and politics" merge in these cities and why segregation by class and race continues to be the order of the day all over America.

LAND DEVELOPMENT: IMPLICATION AND APPLICATION

The pervasive whiteness of land development and "developers" is best understood by tracing some aspects of how it is applied and what is then implied before, during and after that application. As a black man I see the reality much differently than the fluff-piece type definitions that you find in urban planning texts and related resource manuals. I now share those views and analyses with you, the reader.

Here's a sample situation of what takes place behind closed doors while the vast majority of the American public goes back and forth to work, saves their pennies and hopes like hell to save enough to get away from low-income people and minorities. Pressured by "family values" and the mythical "American Dream," the situation is made worse by peer pressure where white families compete with one another based on who has the most prestigious address, lives the closest to the suburban lifestyle and who can be the first to have a three-car garage and a pool in the back yard.

The developer finds out which properties will be considered for some type of major long-range plan – suburban developments, malls or perhaps an interstate coming through an area. Then, these developers form a consortium and put together enough capital to purchase the properties that are in the way of the "master plan." They buy up these properties and then turn around and sell them to the city, the county or whomever has the "master plan" on their desk.

On the other hand the "development" might be an expressway that is being planned and if that is the case, then the Federal government is right there with a blank check, ready to pay whatever is needed (usually sharing costs with local municipalities) to get the freeway built. And it is here where low-income areas suffer the most because they are the ones whose houses will be razed and whose populations will be relocated or transferred to another part of the city.

If the development is an interstate, the developers and potential contractors know what the configuration of the roadway will be. They have to because they have to avoid the white areas (read: voters) and cleave their way through the ghettos, barrios and other low income areas. Scores of communities and towns have been destroyed and bulldozed in the name of Eminent Domain and "the public welfare" by these groups of power-mad white boys whose main concern is getting their race members to and from the airport or downtown jobs on time.

The key is to prevent and screen anything remotely resembling "minority input."

Screening or vetting is one way the lily-white development industry has maintained itself. Through mandatory licenses and certifications, high cost of classes and other forms of racial vetting, they can also use one's past record. In a nation where the overwhelming majority of inmates are brown or black, the screening process can determine who can get involved in real estate development and who cannot. Although the original "crooks" were white and the thievery of most of the land has been completed by Anglos, once in power they make sure others cannot follow suit.

BACKGROUND CHECKS AND VETTING

Certifications and licensures of various kinds continue to screen out nontraditional populations. This is all by design even as those who are a part of the development apparatus continue to pilfer, manipulate and steal land at an unabated rate.

A website called Real Estate Express contains and article under the heading, "Will a Felony Conviction Prevent Me From Getting a Real Estate License?" Here is what I know: where there is discretion in the hands of white men or women there is going to a biased pendulum. Depending on their mood at the time, the pendulum may swing in favor of an application or against that applicant.

Let's go through this article and interject the variable of "race" and see what we can conclude as it relates to the "developer-related" industry in present-day America.

The article begins, thusly:

> Earning a real estate license is a fantastic way to embark on a new career path with unlimited income potential. And taking online real estate courses can be more convenient than any other college course or job certification program. Many real estate schools offer classes online, which means you can complete your real estate training from anywhere. (Real Estate Express, 2018)

Remember that when people write this kind of statement, they are targeting a certain demographic. As a former copywriter for Mutual of Omaha, I wrote that "junk mail" that you receive and immediately toss. In order for you to get people to even read a presentation like this, you have to begin with bullshit. And as you can see, the previous paragraph – like most of the people who aspire to be developers – is full of it.

For instance, a "fantastic way to embark on a new career"? And it has "unlimited income potential"? Doesn't all this depend on your location, your market and the people you work for or who work for you? Of course it does. Real estate schools charge tuition and stretch out over months and sometimes years what can be covered in a week by a skilled urban planner/developer. That is what American education is all about: tuition is a revenue stream. So promise the student a job at the end of the rainbow and you can dupe him/her into doing whatever it takes – including paying for expensive-ass textbooks and other "related materials." Again, cost is a key way to screen out low-income and minority applicants.

Let us continue:

> For people who are looking for a new start with a new career, real estate is an excellent option. But what about those who need a new start from a less-than-perfect past? For someone who has had a felony conviction or other questionable action in their background, **the answer is that you can get a new start if you want to make the change.** (Real Estate Express, 2018 – emphasis added)

Of course everybody wants to "make the change." But it is not up to the felon or the violator alone; it relies on people who are of the same racial stripe as the people who govern, license and make the rules for the developers. The organizations are lily-white as are the associations, networks, and boards of directors. Getting a new start is, once again, a matter of white discretion and today's pervasive whiteness didn't get that way because of any believe in "diversity," "multiculturalism," "inclusion" or "community engagement" by the development folk.

The information website further adds,

> **Disclosure of your felony conviction**
> No matter what state you want to start your new real estate career in, **one of the most important traits looked for in a potential real estate licensee will be good character.** You will be asked to disclose any actions that may have been deemed unprofessional or illegal, with or without a felony conviction. Disclosing this information **does not necessarily disqualify you for licensure**. On the other hand, a failure to disclose information about any such behavior, with or without any felony conviction, **will most likely lead to a denial of license**. (Real Estate Express, 2018 – emphasis added)

The key words above are "does not necessarily disqualify you for licensure." What does that mean? It means "it may or it may not." With such nebulous terminology that translates to mean one thing: white discretion will win out. There will be "exceptions" and then they may make you jump through hoops to show you are qualified, but the underlying assumption is that the people who are already a part of the real estate game are forthright, honest and of high moral character. Nothing could be further from the truth.

This mythical morality is echoed in the following passage:

> **Integrity, honesty, and trustworthiness are all crucial in the real estate industry.** Those individuals that earn a real estate license are

> certified by the state that **they are licensed in to meet certain obligations and responsibilities to their clients and customers**. Among these responsibilities are **honesty and full disclosure**. These are traits that one must exhibit before they will be permitted to take the licensing exam in any state. (Real Estate Express, 2018 – emphasis added)

But what about AFTER the exam? Where are the mandates that prevent restrictive covenants that prevent rentals or sales to people of color or women who have children? Where are the rules that outlaw and ban segregated "communities of interest"? Nowhere to be found. Because these come AFTER you've got the license. Where were these rules when banks were redlining and steering minority applicants? Where were these rules when racial segregation was the law of the land? These rules UPHELD these actions and they still do. Developers and real estate related personnel are in charge of land use and they use it to manipulate and control the population. And they use their profits to promote political longevity. More on that later.

Sometimes newcomers or those who are skeptical or lack confidence will see certain buzz words or phrases and drop out of the application process from the get-go. These include the words "determination," "felony" and "past activities." If you are being disproportionately surveilled, patrolled, stopped, harassed, arrested, frisked and jailed then that goes on your record. If you are white these things are less likely to happen to you. But if you are a person of color, these actions constitute a key in the vetting process. False morality by decision makers and a "record" on the part of the applicant means, as they say in baseball, "You're outta dare!"

Moving right along:

> **Determination of your character**
> How an individual applicant's character is **determined varies from state to state.** All states will ask for the information to be disclosed on the application to sit for the real estate exam. **Some states will require fingerprinting or other background check and the information will be compared to what you disclosed on your application**. Regardless of how the state that you are in requests the information, **you must completely and honestly disclose any conviction, felony or misdemeanor, to ever be considered for a real estate license.** (Real Estate Express, 2018 – emphasis added)

Doesn't this sound totally unorganized? Which states determine what and which ones don't? Is there a regional trend to the ones that are more stringent? Where is the data on which areas are turning down minority and female applicants?

Who is passing that exam and who is not? Who are the ones who are cheating to get by and who, once they pass the exam, engage in activity that is illegal, immoral and unethical?

The information concludes as follows:

> **A felony conviction is a very serious offense, but it is possible to have a new start.** The first step is integrity. **You must display the necessary characteristics of honesty and full disclosure that are required to be a real estate agent in order to be considered to take the real estate licensing exam**. If a person exhibits these qualities, has paid their debt to society, and is completely honest about any felony convictions on their record, **they could** get the opportunity to start over with a prosperous new career in real estate. (Real Estate Express, 2018)

There are no guarantees of anything even after you go through the degradation ceremony outlined above. You COULD get the OPPORTUNITY to start over. You can start over but will your reputation proceed you. Those white boy realtors play dirty, and if they have to pay someone to reveal your record, no matter how insignificant, and it gives them an edge, they are going to do it. The real world is full of these hyper-competitive real estate types.

Vetting for qualifications is the white man's way of DISQUALIFYING people of color. History bears this out time and time again.

DEVELOPERS: TOWARD A DEFINITION

One source offers an operational definition of the function of the real estate developer, also known as the property developer:

> **Real estate development, or property development, is a business process, encompassing activities that range from the renovation and re-lease of existing buildings to the purchase of raw land and the sale of developed land or parcels to others.** Real estate developers are the people and companies who coordinate all of these activities**, converting ideas from paper to real property** … Real estate development is different from construction, **although many developers also manage the construction process.**(Peiser & Peiser, 2003)

From paper to real property. That is how America has controlled the land and the people who live on it. Developers have worked with the construction industry and city administration to buttress racial segregation when it was the *de jure* law of the land up until and including now, while it is the *de facto* law of the land.

Land and the control of it – known simply as "land use" – is in the hands of these people and the average person in America isn't paying any attention until abuse of the real estate method affects them, personally. According to Wikipedia, (2018):

> **Developers buy land, finance real estate deals, build or have builders build projects, create, imagine, control, and orchestrate the process of development from the beginning to end …** Developers usually take the greatest <u>risk</u> in the creation or renovation of real estate—and receive the greatest rewards. Typically, developers purchase a tract of land, **determine the marketing of the property**, develop the building program and design, **obtain the necessary public approval and financing**, build the structures, and **rent out, manage, and ultimately sell it.** (emphasis added)

The role of the developer is usually intentionally undermined when it comes to the public. They keep a low profile in public and reserve their ideas and recommendations to behind closed door meetings with city officials and other politicos. Many of them "throw the rock and hide the hand," as the saying goes.

Look at what they have the power to do as laid out in the previous excerpt: buy land, finance real estate boards, build projects, and orchestrate the process of development from beginning to end. All of his involved capital, financing and hard cash. This means that developers work hand in hand with banking interests and other investment entities and lenders. In historical terms, they were all in on it when the compartmentalization, isolation and systemic impoverishment of the ghetto and barrio were created. They knew ahead of time and, with their role in the city's "master plan" made racial and residential segregation a reality.

The power of the developer should not be understated or ignored:

> Sometimes property developers will only undertake part of the process. For example, **some developers source a property and get the plans and permits approved before selling the property with the plans and permits to a builder at a premium price**. Alternatively, a developer that is also a builder may purchase a property with the plans and permits in place so that they do not have the risk of failing to obtain planning approval and can start construction on the development immediately. (Wikipedia, 2018 – emphasis added)

Or they can get together with the city planning department, plot out and then plan to get a property, parcel it out to their pals who are in the construction industry and in that way, everybody can get a piece of the pie in both the short and long term. Renters and buyers pay without knowing about the money already made with their tax dollars and if they miss a payment, out they go and in comes another sucker …. Oops! I mean customer who is looking for a place to live.

It's all about white nationalism with a token negro presence thrown in every once in a while in order to comply with real or perceived affirmative action needs. Tokenism means that the minority input is nothing more than a shill for the city and the developer, answering only when asked pre-arranged questions and speaking only from scripts that have been provided. In exchange these tokens get to wear suits, attend meetings (after the whites only "pre-meeting meeting has taken place) and then march out to the community and make it appear as if it is "your best interests" that are at the root of the incoming project.

Put another way,

> **Developers work with many different counterparts along each step of this process**, including architects, city planners, engineers, surveyors, inspectors, contractors, lawyers, leasing agents, etc. In the Town and Country Planning context in the United Kingdom, 'development' is defined in the Town and Country Planning Act 1990 s55.(Wikipedia, 2018 – emphasis added)

All of those counterparts are white and totally devoid of any cultural competency. That is why what they produce is white on the outside and white on the inside and then it is IMPOSED on minority communities. When it doesn't fit, the population is blamed, not the poor fit of the project itself. The key to the lily-whiteness and pervasive Eurocentric modeling of development is that it is maintained through what is called the "credentialization process." According to once source,

> Many aspects of the real estate development process require local or state licensing, such as acting as a real estate broker or sales agent along. **A real estate developer is not a professional designation**, there are no schools or associations who recognize or protect the term as a trademark. **Some real estate developers, often those involved in marketing properties through traditional real estate channels, choose to join business associations** (Wikipedia, 2018 – emphasis added)

What then is the definition of a "developer"? A developer of the land is someone who could care less about certain parts of the city. And these are the ones he will venture into because you can buy low and then sell high. He would not dare encroach upon his own gated suburban community. Instead, in the guise of some "special program," some "urban management project" (which I address later) these white men and women with six figure salaries sit in meetings and draw pictures of the ways that they can impact upon the lives of the poor while at the same time generating a profit.

In other, simpler terms, a developer is a pirate and manipulator of land use. Let's take a brief look.

Land Use Law: The Reality of It All

As the recipient of a fellowship from HUD, I attended the University of Iowa's Department of Urban/Regional Planning to work on a Master's degree in Urban Planning. It would have been my second third master's. I did not complete the program but I learned so much from some of the most skilled urban planners in this country, including Dr. Peter Fisher and Dr. Mickey Lauria. I also enrolled in a course in Urban Law.

These classes piqued my interest and I was able to expand upon the master's work I already had in Urban Studies from the University of Nebraska. The point I am making here is that I learned a great deal about land use law, from the classic case of Euclid v. Ambler Reality to the more recent cases involving issues of Eminent Domain, code enforcement and zoning. I began studying on my own and now I have written several books including my most recent one which includes the development of a planning model which I call "The Africentric Sociourban Planning Paradigm."

The point being made here is that when I formed my concern about land use I ran head first into city-run planning departments that were committed to one thing: large paychecks and grant writing to secure more paychecks. What they knew about land use was minimal and much of it was provided to these city planners by local developers and contractors who were rolling in money and had connections with huge construction companies.

This is the reality of land use law when stripped of its pomp and rather impious ceremony. Information provided in this area is largely of the "this great planner said that" and "that planner developed this." But as far as it relates to grass roots issues and concerns, this book is about the defense and development of low-income areas.

Following then is a kind of primer on land use and where the everyday man and woman actually fit in. I shall try to be brief.

One source explains,

> Purchasing unused land for a potential development is sometimes called speculative development. Subdivision of land is the principal mechanism by which communities are developed. **Technically, subdivision describes the legal and physical steps a developer must take to convert raw land into developed land.** Subdivision is a vital

> part of a community's growth, determining its appearance, **the mix of its
> land uses,** and its infrastructure including roads, drainage systems,
> water, sewerage, and public utilities.(Wikipedia, 2018)

And through this you can further determine where certain groups of people will be "steered". Where there are hazards, toxic issues like warehouses and factories or water that could flood an area, that is where these planners and developers work together to promptly place black people and others deemed "social pariahs." Subdivision does more than physically cut up an area; it also parcels out the "good land" from the land that is "more difficult to be developed", with the developers and planners preferring the former while the latter may well constitute one of those areas where new-arriving immigrants and others may be "steered" to live in.

The previous excerpt deals with the "technical" aspects of speculative development. But don't get it twisted; even before all that legal mumbo-jumbo is bandied around in behind closed doors meetings, these old white men are considering where they are going to "place" certain classes and races of people and which zoning laws will ensure residential dwelling, commercial dwelling and mixed-use residency.

Continuing:

> Land development can pose the most risk, but can also be the
> most profitable technique **as it is dependent on the public sector** for
> approvals and infrastructure and because it involves a long investment
> period with no positive cash flow.(Wikipedia, 2018 – emphasis added)

The public sector is quite easy to manipulate because it has already been parceled off and is under the control of white power brokers. The public sector has interlocking directorates and networks where these people communicate along racial lines with both short- and long-term visionary plans that don't include making life better for the poor or minority. That is where the profits come in: segregation is big business and the whiter and area, the more value is given to the land in that area. The more value of the land, the more money that can be made from what is built on that land. Elementary, my dear Watson.

Once the speculative development has been placed on paper and maps and the various "boards," "civic groups," "commissions" and the like are formed, made up of the leading individuals from the public sector, on-going domination of an area can take place:

> After subdivision is complete, **the developer usually markets the land
> to a home builder or other end user,** for such uses as a warehouse or

shopping center. In any case, use of spatial intelligence tools mitigate the risk of these developers by **modeling the population trends and demographic make-up of the sort of customers a home builder or retailer would like to have surrounding their new development**. (Wikipedia, 2018 – emphasis added)

Now you better understand the gradual nature of capital accumulation and the systematic exclusion of people of color. Let me break down the previous passage in terms that are more socially understandable.

The developer and the home builder (contractor) are in cahoots from the outset. They decide what will go where and how much money can be made from such a placement. It is only after the physical configuration has been determined that the speculative development begins to see the light of day. From there comes the lure of the people with money and that means gated communities, condos and huge houses. Surrounding the development with the well-to-do guarantees long term financial support for the malls and other profit-generating structures that will be put in place.

This is the core of the segregationist reality. It may lead to a sector model type box surrounding a box type development form with small businesses supporting each entity, or a sector model type form with several large contiguous areas linking up with each providing special goods and services (e.g., "the restaurant district," "the arts district," "the industrial tract," "the docks," etc.) or it may take the shape of a target, known as "concentric model." Right in the middle is the central business district, surrounding that are expensive homes, around those may be more businesses or leisure activities and way on the outside are the low-income and minority communities.

This is as simple as I can make it because I want the reader to learn, not just be enamored, by what goes on with these developers and their relationships with city planners, contractors and as you will see, various aspects of city government including the mayors.

A key component are the "whites-only" managers, supervisor and consultants who steer and get paid mega-bucks to ensure that the urban area remains under the control of the developers, the city administration, the contractors and the various boards and commissions that serve as "inputs." One such entity is called "Urban Development Management."

CASE STUDY: URBAN DEVELOPMENT MANAGEMENT

Their website spells out both the mission and the vision of this management group, hereafter referred to as UDM:

> UDM concerns the art of managing the decisions of the many stakeholders involved in the development of urban areas towards a high quality outcome—urban places to be enjoyed by all. Chaired by prof. dr. E.M. (Ellen) van Bueren, Urban Development Management is a distinct domain of research and education within the MBE department of the Faculty of Architecture and the Built Environment.

The "managing of decisions," decisions that have already been made by the various boards and commissions – known as "stakeholders".

Following is what UDM is about. To begin with is its international consulting entity that is global in scope, but its functions are essentially the same:

> UDM research helps government authorities, property developers and other organisations to understand and meet key urban challenges like economic transformation, energy transition, climate adaptation, demographic change, and the emergence of big data, smart city solutions, and the circular economy. (van Bueren, 2018)

Notice the triumvirate that is mentioned - "government authorities, property developers and other organizations." You can believe that those other organizations have large budgets that are big enough to commission UDM for whatever "research" may be needed.

Here is where the racism comes in; it's where the claim is made that UDM "understand and meet key urban challenges" and then among those challenges are "economic transformation" but the key is "demographic change." In other words racial and demographic "transitions" and how to prepare for and control a change in the racial character of a given area. I wonder how many minorities they have on staff, or if it's just a bunch of white people sitting around a huge table with demographic data that was gathered by other white people? The claim is that "smart city" solutions are also a part of what is offered by UDM, but you can look at the state of the cities in America and see how divided, disrupted, racially distorted and uncontrolled they seem to be.

The white man is always the "expert," the "authority" and the "advisor" even in those areas where he is totally bereft of knowledge. He wings it and in far too many cases, he gets away with it. He can skim a book or an article before a meeting, highlight key passages, commit key terms to memory and then come out and bloviate about issues that he is actually ignorant of. And because he is speaking to others who are equally ignorant, he gets away with it. Remember that "on the island of the blind, the one-eyed man is king."

What are those "research themes" that these experts specialize in? Well,

> Each member of the UDM team also **specialises in one or more specific research theme(s),** such as mega-event strategies, **waterfront development in seaport cities**, private sector-led **urban development projects, and urban icons and catalyst effects.** (van Bueren, 2018 – emphasis added)

Every single one of these "themes" involves race and class in some capacity. They physical aspects of the projects are named and are of general importance. But believe you me they are all about racial configurations, isolation, relocation or some aspect of "what to do about the niggers." What me to prove it? Okay, let's take each of the following areas: (1) waterfront development in seaport cities, (2) urban development projects, (3) urban icons and catalyst effects.

Waterfront Development in Seaport Cities

Waterfront development is a generic cover for "riverfront development" , but it means essentially the same thing. Cities with a coast line or a water way of some kind want to develop shops, housing and amenities along the shore. The key is to make sure that if there is housing, it will be priced high enough so that marginal people (blacks, low income, others) won't be able to afford to get in. In other words, every waterfront project is a "getaway" or some kind of "local vacation" for the white people in a given city.

Following are a few random selected examples of the power of the waterfront/riverfront and its relationship to business, shops, tourism and freakishness and frolic. According to a plethora of sources, following are examples from a publication called *Coastal Living*:

> Back in the 1960s and '70s, Baltimore and Boston began transforming their blighted industrial **waterfronts into reimagined centers of commerce, dining, and tourism.** This spawned a movement, **and many other old ports have since followed in their ambitious path.** They have now also **included a world class National Aquarium** (Millburg, 2018 – emphasis added)

Notice the transformation of the "industrial waterfront" in two different cities? They saw profits and it surely didn't come to mind from some politician sitting in city hall. It was proposed, in both cases, by the developer and the planners. Add to that the money that was paid under the table to get "priority consideration" for the plans, and the two cities have been making money ever since – from their respective waterfronts. Add to that the internationally-known aquariums, and you have a year round tourism treat, which is why Omaha has added a similar aquarium to its world renowned zoo.

> Camden, Maine - Boaters may grumble about navigating among all the anchored watercraft in Camden's long, narrow harbor. But that layout makes this a wonderful place **for landlubbers to watch the bustle up close.** Spectators can relax amid the greenery in **beautiful Camden Harbor Park.** They can savor some clam chowder or sip wine at one of the restaurants—including The Waterfront—**that perch at the water's edge.** (Millburg, 2018 – emphasis added)

So there you have it: rest, relaxation and restaurants, all so that people can watch the water and the activity along the waterfront. But putting together one of these projects is no easy task: the developers charge big bucks to work up schematics and maps and guidelines for contractors to follow. This is a job for major construction companies and everybody gets paid. We already know that the construction industry is one of the most discriminatory when it comes to hiring blacks. It is simpler and chapter to hire Mexican labor that you can under pay and then threat with deportation if they dare to complain about anything.

> Charleston, South Carolina - Charleston possesses so many historic attractions that some consider it a giant museum, frozen in time. In fact, dozens of huge, modern cargo ships load and unload here every day. **The city provides lots of terrific vistas for watching them (as well as pretty sailboats and other more-playful vessels).** Some of our favorites**: Battery Park, Charleston Waterfront Park, and the wonderful** South Carolina Aquarium; (Millburg, 2018 – emphasis added)

Parks are family-friendly and when people come out they spend money. With the jacked up prices as those eateries along the waterfront, there is plenty of money to be made as the spectators watch the ships load and unload. The parks continue to come into the area and add to the tourist industry.

> Destin, Florida - Amid the high-rises, the outlandishly themed minigolf courses, and all the other resort-town enticements that have proliferated

> in the past couple of decades, the hardworking heart of the "world's luckiest fishing village" still beats at the harbor. Fine-dining restaurants and rollicking bars predominate these days, **but Destin's Old Florida heritage also lives on at such classic no-frills joints as** Dewey Destin's Seafood. **Near the harbor entrance, just north of the bridge, boaters congregate at the submerged Crab Island for a continuous floating party that lasts all summer** (Millburg, 2018 – emphasis added)

Maximum options and entertainment, all along and around the waterway. The waterfront pays for itself after a few years.

> Gig Harbor, Washington - This lovely, slightly rustic town at the south end of Puget Sound **lets you stay overnight in the harbor—on a docked houseboat**. Once a busy center for commercial fishing, boatbuilding, and lumber, Gig Harbor lives a quieter life these days. **It draws steady recreational-boat traffic, so lots of restaurants, shops, and land-based lodging cluster within walking distance of the docks.** Mount Rainier makes a glorious backdrop (Millburg, 2018 – emphasis added)

With Mount Rainer as a view, what waterfront could possibly go wrong? With lodging as a factor, it is clear that this is more of a family or romantic getaway than outright recreation. But this was all in the plans, with new arrivals in terms of eateries and recreation probably continuing to add themselves to the venue.

> Ketchikan, Alaska - This rugged frontier town hadn't changed all that much since Gold Rush days—until massive cruise ships started calling here a few years ago. **The ship-borne influx of gentility (and money)** smoothed out some of Ketchikan's rough edges, **though history** still feels as palpable as the frequent rains. Totem Heritage Center, for example, displays totem poles retrieved from abandoned villages. Many buildings stand on pilings over the water, a consequence of steep hills and the lack of flat land. **Those hills also contribute to the profound, soul-nourishing natural beauty that greets the eye in every direction** (Millburg, 2018 – emphasis added)

Again, ambience is an important additive attraction when you're talking about waterways as the central element of an area. This means that tourism will use that waterway as a lure for outsiders to visit. There is no doubt that the "ship-bourne influx of gentility (and money) generate major profit for the area as a tourist attraction and though not mentioned, there is no doubt in my mind that lodging also offers a huge chunk of revenue.

> Pillar Point, Half Moon Bay, Califor8 - **This marina south of San Francisco strikes a perfect balance between the practical and the picturesque.** The commercial fishing fleet remains strong—and provides great opportunities to buy Dungeness crab and other seafood right off the boat at bargain prices. **Some terrific restaurants** (Barbara's Fish Trap, Ketch Joanne's Restaurant and Harbor Bar, Princeton Seafood Company Market and Restaurant**) and a charming inn** (Oceano Inn Suite**) allow visitors to enjoy the views and the marine life** (Millburg, 2018 – emphasis added)

When I was in high school at Pacifica High in Pittsburg, California, our gifted and talented course would take a junket … oops! I mean "educational field trip" to Half Moon Bay.

Finally And who won the Best American Riverfronts in 2014. According to a publication called Coastal Living, here's the top ten:

1. Wilmington, N.C.
2. Spokane, Wash.
3. Davenport, Iowa
4. Dubuque, Iowa
5. Pittsburgh
6. Louisville, Ky.
7. Chattanooga, Tenn.
8. Savannah, Ga.
9. Detroit, Mich
10. Richmond, Va.

Another variable that has to be considered when it comes to waterfronts is what "community" is going to have to be moved or relocated to make way for some of the projects. These waterfronts will be priced high enough to ensure that few if any minorities will be able to avail of what is being offered and that is surely true if that waterfront also includes condominium or high-rise apartment living.

So UDM can "help" with getting this together – with no mention of race or class? With no references to the geo politics since many of those riverfronts are contiguous to black communities? That's where the white planners and developers "steered" black people to when we initially migrated to their cities – straight to the waterfront where the toxicity, pollution, hard life and potential danger from floods all reigned. So if there is going to be some kind of transformation, then what is UDM going to do? Hold a cocktail party featuring ribs and watermelon? Tacos and enchilada salad? Please!

Urban Development Projects

What do they mean by "urban development projects"? Well without a doubt these are projects that deal with the city and in more than a few cases, probably the central city/urban core.

A website called "BizFluent" offers an excellent overview of the areas that constitute "urban development." According to Brooks (2017),

> Large cities, towns and even small neighborhoods do not spring up overnight. They are the result of careful planning by civil and design engineers, project managers, architects, environmental planners and surveyors. The integration of these disciplines is known as urban development. Urban development is a system of residential expansion that creates cities. Residential areas are the primary focus of urban development. Urban development occurs by expansion into unpopulated areas and/or the renovation of decaying regions.

Urban development in the hands of the white man entails a great deal of anguish on the part of low-income and minority people. In the early days he called it "slum clearance" and then of course came urban renewal which became known in the ghetto as "negro removal." Then you had Model Cities and Enterprise Zones, both of which made white developers and "planners" rich at the expense of the poor. This is an ongoing patterns with these urban renewal projects because the talk is always of "cooperation." But what is taking place today took place in the 1930s and before and was explained by the late Dr. Carter G. Woodson as follows, as he described inter-racial "cooperation". Woodson put it this way:

> Cooperation implies equality of the participants in the particular task at hand. On the contrary, however, the usual way now is for the whites to work out their plans behind closed doors, have them approved by a few Negroes serving nominally on a board, and then employ a white or mixed staff to carry out their program. This is not interracial cooperation. It is merely the ancient idea of calling upon the "inferior" to carry out the orders of the "superior." To express it in post-classic language, as did Jessie O. Thomas, "The Negroes do the 'coing' and the whites the 'operating'" (Woodson, 1933: p. 29).

And that is the way it continues on today, with white folks buying off the land, doing all of the planning, and then doling out a few crumbs to token Black leadership who, in turn, dupe and control the masses of people.

A key cog in urban development is what planners refer to as "natural expansion." According to Brooks (2017),

> **Population growth in major cities requires expansion**. Urban
> developers look to neighboring natural territories **to build needed
> housing and recreational areas.** Natural expansion is the creation of
> residential areas in undeveloped or underdeveloped regions. Natural
> expansion requires the **destruction of the wilderness.** However, urban
> planners must work closely with environmental protection agencies to
> ensure that protected wildlife and plant life are not destroyed. (Brooks,
> 2017 – emphasis added)

The wilderness?! Let's talk about the villages in those areas that have to be relocated or razed. Let's talk closer to home and the black communities that were divided and dissected so that white people could have an interstate. The statement that "population growth in major cities requires expansion" is misleading. It requires expansion for the groups with the money to move into those "new areas." And that means suburbia, exurbia – and white folks.

Developers and planners don't think about expanding the ghetto or the barrio. In fact, with development of expansion for white folks comes increased population density and compartmentalization for people of color. As density goes up so does the likelihood of conflict and that means more overtime, more weaponry and more Federal and state grants for the cops. Can you now see the real role of the developer?

But it doesn't stop there. Brooks explains what is meant by "urban renovation":

> **In extremely populated areas natural expansion is not always
> possible**. If a large city is surrounded by other cities, there is no place for
> the larger city to expand into. **In this case urban planners look to
> renovate decaying neighborhoods, obsolete industrial districts, and
> other unused spaces**. On a much larger scale than natural expansion,
> **urban renovation requires the compliance of city-dwellers**. City
> planners and urban developers **carefully consider the needs of the
> population in renovating urban areas.** (Brooks, 2017 – emphasis
> added)

That last sentence is a damnable lie. But first there are several other points that are in need of correction and clarification.

To begin with, where expansion is not possible the claim is made that planners "look to renovate decaying neighborhoods … and other unusual spaces." The question is how does renovation improve density and lead to expansion? The answer is that it doesn't. That is where the compartmentalization that I wrote of earlier comes in. If they can't spread it up, they head to the skies with high-rise buildings, multi-unit apartment structures. In that way you can maintain the low-income area and its isolation while actually increasing the density in the area in question. In some cases they refer to this as "public housing," but in some cases it is just developers "designing" the urban living spaces, complete with minimal square footage.

Secondly, the claim that "urban renovation requires the compliance of city dwellers." No it doesn't! These white people have been circumventing the input of the poor for centuries! Even when required by grant sources like the Community Development Block Grant, the city administrators meet with the developers and contractors and the city planners sponsor a mock forum where they tell the city dwellers that is coming, not what they want from them! In other words, they just need to show that an attempt was made to "meet with" the folk to be affected, not that they actually listened to them!

Do you have any idea how much money it would cost if input was actually accepted? It would be "back to the drawing board" time and time again and that would take time and in America, time is money. No. They want to keep it simple: one meeting, serve them some food, pacify them with a hi-tech presentations (e.g., PowerPoint) and have them out of there by sundown. If possible, schedule the meeting during times when the working class is at work. This is the reality – don't hate the messenger!

Finally we come to the damnable lie that I mentioned earlier where the claim was made that, "urban developers carefully consider the needs of the population in renovating urban areas." Where did this lie come from and why was the word "carefully" interjected into the truth-claim? This is for social courtesy and the value of the reader of this message. Once the white man's mind is made up about "urban expansion," it goes straight to paper, to maps and to developers and contractors who leech for the job with a vulture-like tenacity. This is the reality of so-called "urban development".

<u>Urban Icons and Catalyst Effects</u>

The question is what can be used, that already exists, that can serve as a "catalyst" for on-going manipulation and re-configuration of the urban area? White folks usually want to use recreation and freakishness as the source. But there are other ways. Grodach (2008) offers one of them:

> A long-held urban redevelopment strategy has been the investment in **flagship cultural projects**—large-scale, iconic museums and arts centres that are intended to enhance the city image while catalyzing private sector investment and attracting tourists to the surrounding area. … The research demonstrates that certain urban design characteristics can negatively affect the ability of a project to attract visitors and generate commercial activity. However, at the same time, factors beyond

the local context may be an overriding factor in project outcomes thus calling into question the concept of cultural catalyst. (Grodach, 2008 – emphasis added)

I was brought into Milwaukee, Wisconsin to teach back in 1987 and what I didn't see was the on-going "urban catalyst" that was taking place and being planned all around me.

The first was the Grand Avenue Mall. It was opened five years before I arrived. The 1982 mall had more than 80 stores in it and was three stories tall. People flocked to it because it contained some important shops like JC Penney's, Boston Stores, Marshall Fields, Gimbel's, T.J. Maxx and many more. But that wasn't really the long-range purpose of the mall as an "urban catalyst."

It was the "Riverwalk."

It started with a skywalk to an area east of downtown, a racially segregated area consisting of white corporate types. The riverwalk also linked businesses downtown during the winter months in Milwaukee, which can be brutal. The project has since morphed into a pedestrian walkway along the Milwaukee downtown in Milwaukee. Since that time Milwaukee's downtown and the city has a host of related events that serve as a kind of "urban catalyst" for the city's reputation: there is "RiverSplash," a three-day festival during the summer that was also held along the Milwaukee River in downtown Milwaukee. The event coincided with "SummerFest" which all lent themselves to Milwaukee's nickname of "City of Festivals."

But RiverSplash folded in 2009 due to costs. But along with the creation of "RiverSculpture," the revelation of public art that still remains, it is clear that the Grand Avenue Mall rejuvenated Milwaukee's downtown

In other words, a large project that can be used as a kind of "hub" for on-going urban development is the key. Milwaukee's downtown is lily white and the black population has been pushed to the north and west. Already one of the most racially segregated cities in America, today in 2014 it is even moreso.

With my definitions provided (rooted in the world of the "actual," not the "imagined") we can get back to the claims offered by Urban Development Management, where it outlines the courses that it offers "on all levels of academic education":

- BK6MA3 Beheer en (Her)Ontwikkeling (5 ECTS)
- BK6ON5 Gebiedsontwikkeling (10 ECTS)
- AR2R025 Urban Redevelopment Game: Integrating Planning, Design and Property Development (10 ECTS)
- AR3R010 MBE Graduation Laboratory.

The age old adage teaches us that, "You can't teach what you don't know and you can't lead where you won't go. There is not a single course listed above, or among the graduate level courses that are also offered, that deals with race and ethnic relations, cultural competency, inter-ethnic relations or social stratification. They are white people teaching white people about how to be white and how to remain that way IN SPITE OF the demographic transition taking place (also known as "the browning of America") instead of IN RELATION to it.

And yet the website has the unmitigated gall t make the following claim:

> **All UDM research and education activities are meant to contribute to real solutions for real urban problems.** The UDM team is aware of the context-dependencies that have to be taken into account **when applying generic insights developed through academic research**. Therefore, the team works closely with professionals to translate concepts, principles, and instruments to local practice situations. (van Bueren, 2018)

Bullshit! You can't take a "generic insight" and then downsize or adjust it so that it applies to a totally different cultural and racial context! That is the problem with education today: these white people think that old time thinkers and scholars like Dewey, Wright, Mills, Freud and the like were so universal that the bullshit they propounded applies to today's racial context. No. They are white and there are more committed to whiteness than they are to any "ism."

The claim is further made that "All UDM research and education activities are meant to contribute to real solutions for real urban problems."

First, the qualifier. It doesn't say that All UDM research and education activities actually DO these things. It says that they are "meant to contribute." That contribution could be minor or non-existent. And just because you "mean" to do something doesn't mean that it is going to be accomplished. After all, "the road to hell is paved with good intentions." These white people know one way of life and that is their own. They do not value the cultural history of black and brown people enough to give it anything but short shrift. Look what they did to the First Nation people.

The hour has been well-spent and I have offered more than enough information to show that UDM is simply another white nationalist method and paradigm that perpetuates whiteness in the name of "urban development." The cities of America are black and brown and the suburbs are white. But all the development, razing, relocating, re-configuration and planning are aimed at the areas where people of color live, especially if those enclaves are anywhere close to a riverfront, a waterway or a downtown area.

The type of government makes a small difference but as I hope to show, it is a small group of white men who in all cases form and shape the style of government, from "mayor-council" and "city manager" to "city manager" and "commission." That is why it is so easy for dissect the theories and claims of these scholars; they continue to undermine the variable of racism and the roles that discrimination and greed play in the land speculation and development process. Each government type requires a different set of manipulations, and it is no more difficult or complex than that.

The urban planning history, the real estate process, and overall American track record of land thievery and configuration all speak for themselves. The politics of development and the developers will now be addressed. As a political scientist we learned that, "all politics is local." Now we will clearly understand how and why this is the case.

<u>Government Types and Impact on Race and Urban Development</u>

There are several – some say three others say give - general types of city government: the mayor-council, the commission and the city manager and as we learned in our political science and government classes, these are the pure forms; many cities have developed a combination of two or three of them. That is why the theories advanced by these so-called white scholars are, at best, nebulous. The form of government dictates the numbers of people who will be compromised by developers and no matter what the aim or intent is of the "master plan," the people at the top will make decisions based on what types of strategies and tactics are going to be used by the locals who have the money and resources.

So for the sake of clarity, let's go through the forms of city government and check out how they are, can and will be manipulated by various types of developers, contractors, consultants and others.

First there is the **Mayor-Council** form of government is also known as the **Strong Mayor form**. This is the mostly employed in larger cities but is not the most popular form. It is the mayor who wins office and then has the power to appoint the people who will lead various city departments. While the council passes laws and ordinances and sets the tax rate, the mayor has control over say, the Planning Director because he appointed him and therefore controls his salary. He also controls the Finance Director. With such "juice," the council is often outgunned and outmanned.

Then there is the **City Manager** form of government and it is most popular form of government in America. It is also known as the Council-Manager form of government. This exists in cities where there are serious urban problems that have to be solved with expertise, not necessarily with a vote. In these instances one source explains that, "The answer has been to entrust most of the executive powers, including law enforcement and provision of services, to a highly trained and experienced professional city manager" (University of Gronongen, 1994-2012).

Furthermore the **City (or Council-Manager) Manager** is also known as the City Manager form of government, the council is the legislative body; its members are the community's decision makers. Power is centralized in the elected council, which approves the budget and determines the tax rate, for example. The council also focuses on the community's goals, major projects, and such long-term considerations as community growth, land use development, capital improvement plans, capital financing, and strategic planning. Dallas is one of the largest cities with this form of government. The mayor is elected during an at-large election. The mayor presides at council meetings and is recognized as the head of the city for ceremonial purposes but has no regular administrative duties. (Wikipedia, 2018)

Other Council Manager forms of government include College Station (TX), Phoenix (AZ), Dallas (TX), San Jose (CA), Austin (TX), Fort Worth (TX), Charlotte (NC), El Paso (TX) and Las Vegas (NV). Cincinnati, Ohio also has this form of government and is one of the cities being analyzed in this book.

The council hires a professional manager to carry out the administrative responsibilities and supervises the manager's performance. . If the manager is not responsive to the council's wishes, the council has authority to terminate the manager at any time. In that sense, a manager's responsiveness is tested daily. The City manager form of government is growing in popularity across America. According to one source, "Under this plan, a small, elected council makes the city ordinances and sets policy, but hires a paid administrator, also called a city manager, to carry out its decisions. The manager draws up the city budget and supervises most of the departments. Usually, there is no set term; the manager serves as long as the council is satisfied with his or her work."

Then there is the **Commission** form of city government, which "combines both the legislative and executive functions in one group of officials, usually three or more in number, elected city-wide. Each commissioner supervises the work of one or more city departments. One is named chairman of the body and is often called the mayor, although his power is equivalent to that of his fellow commissioners." (University of Gronongen, 1994-2012)

This form, which is almost defunct, had an interesting history and surely hails back to my statement regarding "small groups of white men" as the catalyst and the formative beginnings of the process:

> **The commission form of city government, also known as the
> Galveston Plan, was devised in Galveston in 1901 and became one of
> the three basic forms of municipal government in the United States.**
> Under the commission plan **voters elect a small governing commission,
> typically five or seven members, on an at-large basis** … The invention
> of the commission plan was a direct result of the Galveston hurricane of
> 1900. An estimated 6,000 lives were lost, and millions of dollars worth
> of property was swept away. Fearful that the island city might never
> recover its prosperity under the leadership of the incumbent city council,
> **a group of wealthy businessmen known as the Deep Water
> Committee** devised a plan to have the governor appoint a commission to
> govern the city during the rebuilding period. (Rice, 2018 – emphasis
> added)

Take note that in Galveston it was the "Deep Water Committee" that came to be rich white boys making decisions. In Houston it was the "8F Crowd." In Memphis it was a group called "Citizens for Progress." And so on: each city had some rich white boys who decided to band together and "direct" or "lead" the city. They were more than land speculators; in many cases they were outright thieves.

Regardless of the name, the concept of "commission" lingers to this day, only for different and more focused reasons. When white people want to impose a decision on the masses they put together a group of big-named white people, usually old white men, and get them together to make the decision. That decision is then imposed on the mayor, perhaps a few members of the Legislature, and others at the political level and that is how decisions, in various areas, get made.

Des Moines, Iowa is one of the largest city with the Commission form of government. Portland, Oregon had one for a long time and a recent election to change to a Council- Manager form was defeated 76%-24% on the May 2007 ballot.

It should be noted that the City Commission "used to be a popular form of government in the early part of the 20th century but dwindled after that, largely replaced by council-manager governments … The commission form provides for the election of three commissioners who function collectively as the city's legislative body and individually as city department heads. The three are elected at-large to fill the specific offices of the commissioner of public safety (who also serves as the mayor), the commissioner of finance and accounting, and the commissioner of streets and public improvements (public works). (Rice, 2018) Although one of the elected commissioners also has the title of mayor, he/she has essentially the same powers as the other commissioners, with no veto power nor any power to direct city administration except within his/her own department. The commission appoints and removes officials by a majority vote. (Rice, 2018)

Finally, the **Town Meeting** form of government where all the town's citizens gather at least once a year to adopt city laws and policies. At this same meeting, a group citizens or an individual is selected to run city operations. *This form of government is only for the smallest of cities.* It is also known as a **Representative Town Meeting** city government and citizens who do not participate in the meeting may still attend.

With this primer out of the way, the point I want to drive home is that each of these forms of government is wide open to bribery and other forms of money changing hands-type scams that bring in the developers and contractors. They have their own methods but let me provide some examples of how it can be done so the myth of the "all-American city" can be stripped of all that pomp and rather impious ceremony and revealed for what it is when it comes to race relations and land use: the will and right of legalized "organized crime" raised by law and social acceptance to the level of sacred observance.

How could it not be? American society was conceived in crime, brutality, lies and bullshit. Once the First Nation people and their morality was brushed aside, the white man took over and created a "New England" or a "Micro Europe: same values, viewpoints, racist tendencies and sexual perversions. The governments were somewhat different because as former oppressors they did not want done to them what had been done in England. So they created a government that would enable them to "do unto others" and this is the answer to all the "crime" and social deviance, political corruption and the like that permeates American cities, from the largest to the hick towns.

It is clear that the mayor-council form is easy to bribe because of the need for an election. Because voters are so important, the people with the power and the constituents can influence the election. Those with the money can make campaign donations that will make the winner indebted to them. This is vintage American politics and it's "hidden in broad daylight." The white majority of this country is too busy working and taking care of maintaining their segregated way of life to worry about outcomes, as long as there is evidence that the person they donate to and support maintains the white way of life with few, if any exceptions.

The Mayor-council form is the perfect foil for developers and contractors. Make promises of a new skyline, new buildings downtown, perhaps a new city hall and if the backing is there, you are in. Once in you don't even have to deliver on the specific promise; but if you want more than one term you can pacify the masses with some huge bricks-and-mortar project that will impress them the same way bright lights and bells impress an infant.

The city manager/council manager form is even easier. The council handles all of the real work but the smart ones usually immediately kowtow and kiss up to the newly elected mayor and deals get cut. The mayor is elected at-large, meaning that it is a popularity contest. The mayor begins meeting with "certain members" of the council and forms a cadre of supporters. That is how power is maintained and that is how developers and contractors get int. Council members make recommendations from their district, take it to the Mayor, the previously formed cadre meets and the developer gets the project. Bid-rigging is a staple of this form of government, which is why architecture-strong cities like Dallas and Las Vegas are filled with corruption and behind-closed-doors dickering.

The Commission form, as mentioned, is for smaller cities. It seems to me that these "smaller cities" are a lot cleaner than the larger ones (I've been to both Des Moines and Portland). With a small commission a fast-talking developer could get in there with a plan and launch a "build, build, build" initiative that might convince most of them. I can see it taking place in Portland and even now the city is recruiting, on line, for investors to come in and look at the available properties in the neighborhoods as well. The group in charge of this is the Downtown Development Group which says that it "represents a large portfolio of property available for development."

As for Des Moines, they too have a group called Downtown Development. The Senior Vice-President has the following to say on his website:

> In a time when many cities seem to be stuck in neutral, Downtown Des Moines (DSM) is experiencing an unparalleled growth spurt. In the past 10 years, $3 billion have been invested in the capital city, with an average of 40 ongoing development projects happening at any given time. It's thanks to numbers like these that Fortune magazine ranked DSM as the #1 Up-And-Coming Downtown in America in 2014.

Finally the even lesser known Town Meeting/Representative forms of government and it should be clear that the fewer people and the smaller the city, the easier it is to fast-talk them and get those developers to offer incentives (bribes) to convince the decision makers that a particular land speculation can reap great benefits. A few people meet once a year or so and then from that group a decision maker is selected. This process is the perfect storm for external forms of control and organized crime.

It should be noted that most of these types of government are found in New England. According to the Encyclopedia Britannica (2018)

> At the meetings, which may be held periodically or on demand, officials and school boards may be elected or chosen to govern between meetings; ordinances may be adopted; and taxes and expenditures may be debated and voted upon. Because of the extraordinary autonomy granted each town, New England state legislatures end up being among the largest in

the United States. (Encyclopedia Brittanica (2018). Retrieved from
https://www.britannica.com/topic/town-meeting)

So there you have it - Government Types and Impact on Race and Urban Development. I would not feel right dishing out the intellectual ass whipping to developers and contractors if I didn't provide sufficient context to show how deeply embedded these contractors, real estate speculators, urban planners, developers and the like are in the problems with urban America and the decay of political independence when it comes to land use.

With this having been done, we can now home in on city leaders and their roles (complicity) in "development and economic concerns" in a particular city.

MAYORS, DEVELOPERS AND ECONOMIC CONCERNS: AN INTRODUCTION

The title of this book is *Rich Developers and African-American Under-Development: The Economic and Sociopolitical Realities of Segregation of American Cities,* and the title carries an explanation of the "ruler and ruled" relationship that is par for the course in America, and has been that way since the Europeans came to this country. Planners and developers worked together to divide up the land, name the cities and streets, and find the financing that would make the streets and lighting better while e making sure to isolate the new immigrants, blacks, Mexicans and Asians beyond the city limits as well as beyond the pale of human understanding.

When I say "rich" there will be people who point to some developers as being middle class or will argue that "they are not rich." My point is that in white America, if you are white, your colorlessness and background give you the status of potential heir to the throne. That is the only logical way, for example, to explain how an asshole like Donald J. Trump could become president. Sure, there are poor whites – but they ain't po' because they're white!

This book is a primer and is aimed at making the masses aware of how their respective city administrations work with developers and contractors to alter the city around the masses of people. The hard working people who drive back and forth on those highways and who see the street lights come on at night have no idea how much money exchanges hands to ensure that these utilities remain intact. More importantly, they don't even seem to care why some people live in gated communities and others, regardless of income, are relegated to a different 'standard' of the American Dream.

The following section consists of a number of hand-picked random examples that are surely representative of what is taking place in cities of various sizes and locations all over America. Omaha, Nebraska has been omitted intentionally because it's high level of collusion, corruption and malfeasance by mayors, city planners and developers has been well documented in my grievances that have been submitted to the Department of Housing and Urban Development over the past several decades. HUD's inaction and outright buffoonery is another reason why so many cities continue to get away with stealing grant money to finance the future of the city and fate of these developers, contractors, and real estate speculators.

The American mayor is constantly on the lookout for new "revenue streams" and the key to that is land use controls. In most cases the issue of race is not mentioned, but because America is so segregated you need not use terms like "slums," "ghetto" "urban core" or "inner city" any more. All you have to do is make reference to a particular zip code, area of town by name of the "neighborhood" and you know if it is white, brown or black. This is the product of the work of the city planners, developers and mayors.

MAYORS, DEVELOPERS AND THE POLITICAL ECONOMICS OF THE CITY

Ehrenhalt (2016) opens up his article, "The Reality of Mayors' Economic Promises" on mayors and economic problems by stating, "They vow to rev up the local economy all the time, exposing their misunderstanding and political office." I don't know if this is all the time accurate, since far too many of the people who run for mayor do so for the power, the money, the perks and the junkets and few really give a damn about the people who voted them in. With that in mind, behind closed-door meetings are par for the course and on some level, what I am about to share with you takes place in every major- and middle-sized city in America.

The article continues from November of 2016 continues:

> Nearly half of America's 100 biggest cities are electing mayors this month, and most of the winners will come floating into office on a tide of promises, some of them achievable **and some so ambitious that the candidates themselves don't have a clue how to pull them off.**
> (Ehrenhalt, 2016 – emphasis added)

The fact of the matter is, based on my more than four decades of community work, that the last sentence in the previous paragraph – that some of the people running for mayor that they don't have a clue how to pull off the promises they make – is the statement that is closest to accurate. I would say that this fits the majority of the candidates.

On the other hand why should they know anything? They run for office because of promises made by powerful people that they will donate money, resources and time to the campaign. All the candidate has to do is be able to bullshit people, look good in a tight and short skirt, and be able to impact on a number of institutions (rather than individuals) which means corporations, nonprofits, churches and educational institutions. That is how elections are won, and the goals are set by the people who are "behind" that candidate, usually people with money.

Furthermore,

> Many will have vowed to be "education mayors" -- school reformers who will generate test results so much improved as to make their communities magnets for the affluent residents they are competing to attract. Candidates make these vows despite decades' worth of evidence **that there is little a mayor can do to produce dramatic educational improvement over the course of a term in office.** (Ehrenhalt, 2016 – emphasis added)

That is why most of them don't take the education route. In many cities the educational system is not linked to the city administration. The mayor's that make references to education are talking about the youth in the schools and what they will do to provide jobs for those youth. They are talking about the educational system as a means of providing resources to communities: swimming pools, access to gyms, track fields and meeting room space for community meetings. The people running for mayor are usually idiots themselves and a direct link to education would put them on the spot and they would be asked "education-related" questions which they could not come close to answering.

Moving on:

> But that's the way it is with political promises. **To attract attention -- and votes -- you're better off promising to do something difficult.** Nobody runs for mayor of a big city vowing to become the "sanitation mayor." Picking up the garbage is something everyone expects you to do. Being exceptionally good at it scores no political points. **It's a task that gets noticed only when it's botched.** (Ehrenhalt, 2016 – emphasis added)

The preceding is only partially true. In far too many cities garbage collection is not only big business but it is a job creator. In a city that has a low educational attainment level, getting hired as a garbage man is a big deal. And this is especially true for people of color. So it is as task that can be used and exploited, especially if you can bring in a minority-owned business to run the garbage collection. If you can do that, then you really don't have to worry about hiring people of color for anything else because you can point at and boast about how you "support minority businesses." This is the reality of the situation.

Despite my profound re-calculation of the earlier claims, the author continues to back his claim as follows:

> The smartest political candidates understand this. They make promises that stand somewhere between the grandiose and the trivial. They look for challenges that, with the requisite amount of intelligence, energy and luck, might be met in a meaningful way. **In the words of George Latimer, who was a highly effective three-term mayor of St. Paul, Minn., these candidates don't chase problems. They chase opportunities**. (Ehrenhalt, 2016 – emphasis added)

George Latimer is mouthing clichés that are only partially true. The fact is that if you "chase problems," you can create opportunities. You don't have to actually SOLVE the problem – just give chase. And that in itself will land you some votes because most people will avoid the problem and give reasons why they don't think that problem can be solved. If you go after it that is a victory of sorts – it shows the kind of bravado that voters view as a sign of strength. Mr. Latimer should keep his mouth shut.

Continuing:

> **For many candidates in 2016 who would like to be as successful as Latimer, the question of what to chase is fairly obvious: economic development**. Promise to lure in the corporations that will provide massive numbers of new jobs and restore (or preserve) the city's economic vitality. Push through tax incentives and other economic subsidies that will make your city look more attractive than the other jurisdictions competing for the same prizes. **Land a few big fish, and you will leave office with the satisfaction that you have done something important**. (Ehrenhalt, 2016 – emphasis added)

To begin with, just because you've been in office for a few terms doesn't mean that you were "successful." Just look at Rob Emmanuel of Chicago; look at Marion Barry of Washington D.C. and for that matter Sharon Pratt Dixon of the same city. Look at Coleman Young and Kwame Kilpatrick, both of Detroit. Look at Wellington Webb of Denver, Colorado and Harry LaRosiliere of Plano, Texas (who I include in this book). Look at Ray Nagin of New Orleans or Mike Boyle of Omaha, Nebraska. All served multiple terms and kissed the asses of big business but what was the determining factor was their immoral and unethical acts once they began to feel their own power. They began to think that they were above the law. And there are many more who prove this point as well.

So it's not just a matter of economic development and luring big business. It's the ability and willingness to kowtow, bow and scrape and do the bidding of these powerful people once you get on board. If you get too big for your britches or you start thinking that you are the one who is really in charge, you are a goner.

Continuing:

> It's an appealing strategy, and it's one that, in much of urban America, is hard to resist. But how successful is it likely to be? How often does any set of public policies deserve credit for a city's economic revival? **When a city's economic fortunes improve in a relatively short time, does that mean the mayor was smart -- or does it just mean that he or she was lucky?** (Ehrenhalt, 2016 – emphasis added)

Again, the wrong questions is being posed. It is not a matter of being smart or lucky. It is a matter of being a good "manager" of what could be called "corporate relationships" or "donor relations." It's makings sure that the powers that be get what you promised them in order to get all that backing and money you received. It is not about YOUR luck or intelligence; it is about your ability to manipulate the power barons that are the key to the financial fate, the revenue streams and the employment status of the city you are mayor of!

Now I will match wits with a law professor and you can see who you agree with:

> Richard Schragger, a **law professor at the University of Virginia**, has taken a look at mayors and economic development strategies in cities all over the country and has come up with a sobering but compelling conclusion: **When the strategies work, it's mostly luck**. "Any claim that a specific policy will foster growth or decline," Schragger says in his new book, *City Power*, "should be treated with a great deal of caution. ... **Confident predictions that economic growth is attainable if city leaders would just get with the program are seriously oversold.**" (Ehrenhalt, 2016 – emphasis added)

You can't run a city based on "luck." That is bullshit. You are a white man and as such, you have to find other white men to keep the city under control and you have to make sure that outsider forces don't come in and cut into the profit margin. The fact that "economic growth is attainable" is a reality that is based on volume of jobs provided and what's the surrounding states are doing. In-migration from other states can be manipulated and used to feed into your economy; annexing of surrounding areas can create debt but also add to the taxes you can collect. These are unpopular manipulations but they are based on skill not luck. An effective office of development (grant writers) can also be a big boost, but you have to be willing to pay for the best people. This is not a matter of luck, but a matter of "intelligent selection."

More from Schragger:

> Schragger's skepticism about economic development politics is grounded in a conviction that most political actors misunderstand what cities are fundamentally about. **In his view, they subscribe to the market-driven ideology that envisions cities as products, vying with each other to present the most enticing offers and attract the most desirable collection of customers -- or corporations**. Schragger, on the other hand, is a disciple of the late Jane Jacobs, and shares the renowned urbanist's long-held conviction that **a city is a bundle of organic processes interacting with each other in myriad ways and much too complex to be understood in simplistic free-market terms**. "We talk about cities as if they were businesses," he writes, "when that is not what cities are at all." (Ehrenhalt, 2016)

This is what I have been saying! *The only difference is that the city is not a product –it is power source.* The people don't make the city – the idea of the city makes the people. From that pride of "belonging" or living in "a city," the people can be manipulated to do whatever it takes to stabilize their own well-being. People boast about the cities they live in all the time and if the tourism department is doing its job, each city has a source symbol: New York is size, Minneapolis is waterways, Texas is country-type fun and games, San Francisco is the open lifestyle and we all know what Vegas is. These are SOURCES that people gravitate toward, not a product. The product is the revenue stream and the finances generated by the city's reputation!

Moving on:

> If cities were businesses or products in competition with each other for sales, Schragger points out, **it would be reasonable to expect that over the past couple of decades the ones prospering most conspicuously would have been the ones offering customers the best deals -- specifically, the juiciest array of tax breaks.** But as we all know, that isn't what happened. Boston, **New York and Seattle are all high-tax cities, and they are all thriving.** Meanwhile, dozens of struggling Rust Belt cities have thrown elaborate tax break bouquets at businesses and

are worse off than they were in 1970. (Ehrenhalt, 2016 – emphasis
added)

Schragger has it ass backwards. The cities that are prospering most conspicuously are the ones that are ranking high in tourism. That means people are visiting and relocating there because of what the reputation of that city is. The "best deal" is ultimately a place to live, somewhere for their kids to go to school and someplace safe. The examples he used, Seattle and New York, are also waterway cities and that helps add to the leisure life that these migrants are looking for. If a corporate is locating to a city, tax breaks are important. But more important is employee satisfaction.

The fact is, people can be programmed to "pay for what you get" and you need only look at the gradual rise in prices of food and services, and the American acceptance of it, to show that attraction to the "source" is the key to a city's growth and its power to be able to impose its public relations will on huge numbers of people and corporations.

Another example used in the article is Boston. Let's see if the illustration is appropriate:

> The most impressive economic development coup in the past couple of years is probably Boston's success at enticing General Electric Corp. to move its headquarters from suburban Connecticut to its downtown waterfront. Of course, **this wasn't accomplished without subsidies**. The city of Boston and the state of Massachusetts offered **nearly $175 million in grants and property tax relief.** But it was far from the best deal on the table. If GE had chosen a new location based only on the financial incentives being offered, it would have done better moving to the suburbs of New York, or perhaps even staying in Connecticut. (Ehrenhalt, 2016)

The end result is the move to Boston, but actually it proves my point. It wasn't the economic incentives in and of themselves. It was Boston as the source. The waterfront was probably a key but Boston is one of America's original and "great" cities. This is a bragging point. With Boston's reputation and history as a source (omitting the fact that it is also one of the most racist), the offer that was made was much more palatable. Boston is not the product – it is the SOURCE of economic development. Reputation is the lure and the magnet that enables corporate America to make decisions like these.

The article continues:

> So what are we to make of the resurgent big cities of the 21st century? What did they do to earn that distinction? If they didn't succeed through

economic development bribery, maybe they did it by electing leaders who were simply better at management than the competition. Schragger acknowledges a grain of truth to this argument, but not much more than that. Looking back over the past generation, it's certainly true that Pittsburgh has benefited from having more capable stewardship than Detroit has had. **Pittsburgh's mayors worked hard to nurture the city's combination of good universities and advanced medical research, rather than making foolish investment decisions and staying yoked to a declining industry.** (Ehrenhalt, 2016 – emphasis added).

Ehrenhalt continues to make my point. Pittsburgh was the source of any economic development, not the product of it. Naturally speaking, you had all those waterways which were then transformed into Three Rivers. Logistically, the waterfront became a sight to behold. World-class hotels then dot the downtown skyline. These are lures that attract corporate America. The schools are a big draw as well because they can train future corporate employees and assist in research. Again, the city's reputation is the magnet that brings corporate America – corporate America does not PRODUCE the city.

Continuing the comparison with Detroit (of all places):

> But when you add up all the factors that led to Detroit's bankruptcy in 2013, it's difficult to say that bad management -- or any particular set of policies -- was the primary culprit. The decline of Detroit was much more complicated and multifaceted than that. It was, in a certain sense, organic. (Ehrenhalt, 2016)

Bullshit. It was race and poor management. It was Kwame Kilpatrick bleeding the city and pilfering money and dividing it up with those big wig financial backers. It was a black city that was unattractive to corporate America because of its blackness. That's why they moved the basketball arena out of Detroit's suburbs ("The Palace") and back into the city, whose reputation was magnified with new development to go with the giant arena, named Little Caesar's Arena:

> The arena features a unique, **glass-roofed concourse connecting it to offices and shops surrounding it.** It anchors a new $2.1 billion 650,000-square-foot (60,000 m2) **sports and entertainment district** in and around downtown Detroit that will include **mixed-use neighborhoods with new residential and retail outlets** located around the Cass Corridor, Ford Field, and Comerica Park. (Wikipedia, 2018)

Detroit is the magnet, originally because of the Ford Motor Company. They lost that magic and tried to go suburban in order to "get away from the niggas." But that was changed after they got rid of Kwame Kilpatrick and the lure of "the city," of "Motown" came roaring back. And as you can see the corporate world is more than large buildings – it also consists of a mixed-use residential environment. The city is the LURE, not the product. In simpler terms, "Build it, and they will come."

Schragger is hung up on the role of education and the creation of better school districts. This is at best tertiary if the city's reputation as an urban center is not in place. For instance, more examples provided by the article:

> Education **might best be** looked at in a similar way. **Every mayor** wants to talk about creating better school systems, but as Schragger points out, **there hasn't been much of a detectable correlation in recent years between educational improvement and broader economic revival.** Chicago and Philadelphia have been burdened for several decades now by dysfunctional school systems, but both have experienced central city comebacks that have spread beyond the immediate downtown area into an ever-expanding network of surrounding communities. (Ehrenhalt, 2016 – emphasis added)

"Every mayor" does NOT want to talk about creating better school systems because most of them are not prepared to do so. In a number of jurisdictions the school system is not even within the city's administrative purview. Schools have their own boards of education and are run by the state. Where in the hell is Shragger coming from? It is equally ludicrous to believe that education al improvements have a DIRECT impact on an economic revival. Education is relative to certain jobs which, in turn, impact on the economy, but other than that Shragger is hailing back to the old days.

The article further claims that,

> **Reduced crime is often cited as a fundamental ingredient of urban recovery, and I would assign it more importance than Schragger does in explaining the success of Boston, New York and, until the last couple of years, Chicago.** The fact remains, however, that crime has declined significantly just about everywhere in America since the 1990s. If safe streets were the secret ingredient of comeback cities, there would be many more of them. **Controlling crime may be a necessary condition for urban revival, but it clearly isn't a sufficient one.** (Ehrenhalt, 2016 – emphasis added)

Now he talks about "fundamental ingredients" to urban recovery. Putting an end to poverty is even more fundamental but I don't see these white city administrators doing a damn thing about that. In fact, they contribute to it with their on-going steering and redlining policies. And they are aided and abetted by local developers and contractors who continue to slice up and eviscerate black and brown areas of town in the name of white upward mobility. So "reduced crime" means starting with the white collar criminals in the city and county administrations and then scaling down from there, including the corrupt cops and their black-on-black murder snitch systems. Only then will you be making a real dent in deviant behavior at the grass roots level.

Ehrenhalt continues his inane stab at urban development:

> **It's tempting at this point to invoke some sort of amenity thesis, such as Richard Florida's much-discussed argument that the successful cities are those that do best at attracting the "creative class" of highly educated young professionals**. General Electric is, indeed, moving to Boston because of some combination of intangible amenities that young talent is looking for; the company's executives have made this very plain. **There seems to exist a mixture of demographics, technology and culture that can constitute a winning formula for cities. But knowing this is not the same as knowing how to create it.** (Ehrenhalt, 2016 – emphasis added).

What the previous statements imply is that college education is the key. That is what is meant by "highly educated." What I have found in my dealings is that the world is filled with "educated fools." To assume that education is the key is to assume that these students, for one thing, did their own homework and research. I know from firsthand experience I wrote more than a hundred term papers. Those kids went on to pass their courses and probably get jobs in the corporate sector. Is this the kind of "highly educated" employee they're talking about.

College education is a bias against minority kids unless the corporate has a quota or is under legal pressure because of the "lack of diversity." If that isn't the case then the corporation will be lily white and once the community finds out that is going to create an entire new list of social problems to deal with.

Omaha, Nebraska's population was so stupid that Con-Agra, after spending millions on a major building and park, packed up and headed to Chicago where there higher intelligence and more diversity. Of course they left the blue collar workers behind n Omaha. The "creative class" of young educated professionals are going to be attracted to big name cities as the "source," as I have cogently contended. The day of the hillbilly is over: these white kids want some "flava" and they sure can't find it among members of their own "vanilla" race. These are simply the facts – don't hate the messenger.

That is why,

> In the 15 years since Florida first advanced his ideas, it is hard to think of a city that has set out purposefully to become a creative-class mecca and actually become one. Urban histories unfold for reasons that are very difficult to understand, as Jane Jacobs knew well and as Schragger argues persuasively. (Ehrenhalt, 2016)

The reason for that is clear: you can't "become" a creative class mecca unless the "source ingredients" already exist, as I have contended. Just as cities with waterways make for good ports and docks, cities with culture and color make for an urban workforce. And an urban workforce is one with experience and more importantly, with "cultural competency." With America's demographics going through a major transition (the "browning" of America), these corporations had better be looking at city's with a "source" that can act as a magnet for intelligent employees from all racial backgrounds. That lily-white shit ain't gonna cut it in the 21st century and beyond.

With that having been established, Ehrenhalt finally asks the question that is on everybody's mind as far as it relates to developers and the political economy of cities:

> **So what should this year's crop of eager new mayors set out to achieve?** Schragger has a simple answer to that question, although it is not one that all of them will wish to embrace. He believes, among other ideas, that they should **set a goal of tempering the inequality that has become endemic to even the most fortunate American cities in recent years.** He wants them to fight for a higher minimum wage, one that would rise in graduated steps to $15 an hour and then beyond it. Raising the minimum wage, he says, is a concrete step that most cities can take and then measure the consequences. In Schragger's view, the consequences will be overwhelmingly positive: If a small number of jobs are lost in the process, they will be more than compensated for by tangible gains for most of the workforce. (Ehrenhalt, 2016 – emphasis added).

Again, Schragger comes over to my side, but again, he falls far short because he is a "racialist" himself. Racialists believe that solutions to issues of inequality can be resolved through economic means. This implies that the problem is one who those who earn more money than others. That is "economic inequality." Before you can get to that point you have to have some semblance of social inequality. That is not attainable in these cities who are so reliant on segregation, redlining and the "steering" of minority populations. And that is why economic equality cannot make a difference because we have moved from "Separate but equal" to "equal but separate." People can have income equality but if you head to the suburbs after work and I head back to the ghetto, what in the hell as really changed?

Again, Ehrenhalt:

> That isn't a practical strategy everywhere. More than a dozen states now restrict the ability of their localities to raise the minimum wage. In those states, Schragger recommends the expanded use of "community benefits agreements" **-- deals with developers that extract concessions on jobs, housing and community services in exchange for land use allowances over which the local government has control**. (Ehrenhalt, 2016 – emphasis added)

"Community benefits agreements" meaning agreements that white people and those in power benefit from. And whose jobs, housing and community services are going to have their concessions taken away? It will be the poor and the "land use allowances" will be the vacant lots, the dilapidated housing and other areas that the city can buy low and sell high. Again, Ehrenhalt doesn't understand the reality of the situation because he is too ignorant (or gutless) to interject the realities of race and how the white man's control of land use based on race is a major determinant in a city's overall quality of life.

The article concludes, thusly:

> By no means is this a comprehensive agenda. It's barely a beginning. But it's built on a recognition that cities would be better off in the long run if mayors and other leaders looked at their capacities more realistically. "Cities," Schragger says, "should do less of what they cannot do … and more of what they can -- provide quality basic services to their residents. … Abandoning local economic development policies is almost politically impossible for local leaders. But it is the right thing to do." (Ehrenhalt, 2016)

Mayors and city leaders, the latter group usually self-proclaimed, handpicked or somehow appointed or "anointed." Indeed, it falls on the backs of the mayor or the city leaders. In any case, they are all power hungry and want to remain in office. They are therefore, for the most part, susceptible to bribery and under-the-table payments. And the developers, contractors and the rest of the "land use gang" is right there with 'em.

New York Mayors Michael Bloomberg/Bill de Blasio and the Developers

Throughout this book I point out the unspoken link between developers, city leadership and the issue of race. This fact is highly visible in some areas and hidden away by others. But make no mistake, it's right there and sooner or later it will manifest itself. As one cultural nationalist once wrote, "A racist is like a dog; you can teach it to stand on its hind legs (being liberal) but it eventually falls back to all fours."

New York is America's crown jewel and no one knows this better than African-Americans in Harlem and the Jews who live everywhere else. It is the most powerful city in the world. It is also one of the most racially and ethnically divided places in America, but as is the case with American cities, the tourism people and others want to hint around that all is good and fair (in total contradiction to American history). At any rate, one song represents this utopian view of "The Big Apple"

Originally performed by Liza Minelli in the film, "New York, New York" in 1977, my favorite version of it is by Frank Sinatra (who crooned it a year later in 1978). At any rate the lyrics are widely recognized as the "anthem" of the city and deservedly so. With so many burroughs and so much land, New York has long been a haven for real estate magnates and land speculators. I will use the lyrics of "New York, New York" as a lead in for this piece on New York Mayor Michael Bloomberg:

Start spreading the news
I'm leaving today
I want to be a part of it
New York, New York

These vagabond shoes
Are longing to stray
Right through the very heart of it
New York, New York

I wanna wake up in a city
That doesn't sleep
And find I'm king of the hill
Top of the heap

These little town blues
Are melting away
I'll make a brand new start of it
In old New York

If I can make it there
I'll make it anywhere

It's up to you
New York, New York

New York, New York

I want to wake up in a city
That never sleeps
And find I'm a number one
Top of the list
King of the hill
A number one

These little town blues
All melting away
I'm gonna make a brand new start of it
In old New York

And if I can make it there
I'm gonna make it anywhere
It's up to you
New York, New York, New York

With the understanding that New York is a hard city to make it in, let's look at who IS making it: the political leadership and the on-going spate of projects that continue to alter the skyline of this beautiful city.

We begin with a December 2013 article from the New York Times for this reason: even when on the way out the door, and Administration still wants a reputation, the glamour and whatever payments can be secured, for its development projects. Let's take a look and see how it was done under the administration of former New York Mayor Michael Bloomberg. The title just about says it all: "Going Out With Building Boom, Mayor Pushes Billions in Projects." Key segments of the article will be analyzed. The article begins thusly:

> The Bloomberg administration has been pushing through more than $12 billion worth of real estate projects in its waning days, trying to solidify the mayor's claim to having transformed the face of New York City and lock in plans before Bill de Blasio takes over Jan. 1. (Bagli, 2013)

In the big cities it's about huge housing developments but more importantly, it's about trying to "change the skyline." Even a hick town like Omaha, Nebraska worked toward that end under the mayorship of Hal Daub. Daub won in a special election in 1995 over real estate magnate (see?) P.J. Morgan and immediately set about changing the skyline of downtown Omaha. He won another term and continued and by the time he was done there were new buildings for Union Pacific, the Omaha World Herald and he laid the groundwork for the First National Bank Tower, which when completed in 2002 was the tallest building in Nebraska

These men about tall buildings because in my view the see them as phallic symbols. But in mega-cities like New York, there are other projects that can generate funding, bring notoriety and also cement your legacy in the ranks of big-time mayors. For instance in the case of Bloomberg,

> The gusher of projects recently approved or on track for approval in Mayor Michael R. Bloomberg's final days include an **outlet mall** and a giant observation wheel on Staten Island, totaling $580 million, and a relatively modest **$16 million building in Manhattan with 55 experimental micro-apartments,** as well as a **$2 billion residential complex on the Brooklyn waterfront** and the country's **largest indoor skating complex, to be built in the Bronx**. (Bagli, 2013 – emphasis added)

Something for everybody – or so it appears on paper. But low income people can afford to go skating, but those micro-apartments and that residential complex on the waterfront are probably for "yuppies" only. The office buildings represent revenue streams but they take time to find companies to lease them. It's all about ego and the financing and the developers get the money and the city gets its share of the loot. The masses of people get nothing but taxes.

Continuing:

> Mr. Bloomberg **has sought to remake the city's landscape for the 21st century,** pushing for **higher-density development** and higher-quality design and opening up the city's vast **waterfront to new residential, recreational and commercial uses.** Nearly 40 percent of the city has been **rezoned** during the mayor's 12 years in office. (Bagli, 2013)

The reason for the re-zoning was in preparation for future plans. Bloomberg was thinking ahead – or should I say the developers he was in bed with were thinking ahead. Bloomberg was just the tool that was being used to make money for the movers and the shakers in the construction industry. Notice above where there is a call for "higher density development." That means apartments and condominiums that will be priced right out of the range of people of color and other low income people who aspire for a better life. The concept of t "pay to play" is not more evident than the housing that you can afford to live in. White developers and city leaders like Bloomberg are well aware of this.

Note also the waterfront utilization – elsewhere in this book I document how waterfronts, riverfronts and lakefronts translate into big bucks for these cities.

Tourism, recreation, the hotel industry, boating-related leisure – all for freakishness and frolic.

They're referred to as "legacy projects" and the reason is pretty obvious. As Bagli (2013) explains,j

> The man spearheading the efforts, the deputy mayor Robert K. Steel, and other officials have made it clear to the City Council, as well as to the real estate and construction industries, that they are determined to finish public reviews **for a number of "legacy projects" before Mr. Bloomberg leaves office.** (Bagli, 2013 – emphasis added)

Furthermore,

> The projects, which will begin construction **well after Mayor-elect de Blasio takes office in January,** also bind the new mayor to the old mayor's agenda, at least for a while. By Dec. 31, some projects, like a $1.2 billion Hudson Yards office tower and a **$1.7 billion Hunter College and Memorial Sloan-Kettering Cancer Center complex**, will have reached the point that they cannot be stopped or modified. (Bagli, 2013 – emphasis added)

These white men band together from all professions. Many of the large cities and several mid-sized ones (e.g., Omaha, Nebraska) will pour money into various "cancer center" and name them after rich white people. In that way they can serve the public good, get paid for doing so and change the skyline and promote the city all at the same time. In Omaha the University of Nebraska Medical Center is expanding all across the mid-town area and in the process is buying up and razing property – including homes and businesses. The University of Nebraska Omaha is doing the same thing to the west of that project in the name of an "Ak-Sar-Ben Village" (Ak-Sar-Ben is Nebraska spelled backwards)

With hospitals and cancer centers come the professionals who will then be able to afford to move into the apartments and condos that will encircle the project. This type of "concentric zone" plan ensures that low-income people will be pushed further and further outside of the "ring" and the only businesses that will survive are those who are grandfathered in or who will be able to afford the predicable spike in rents, lease amounts and other expenditures.

Much of it is for leisure, and the white American is well known for his hedonism. After complaining about how hard they work (those who are able to find jobs in an increasingly technologically-dependent culture), the way to keep the workers from revolting is to pacify them with bullshit activities: skating rinks, professional sports teams to cheer, and so on. But there's more:

> Others, **like a soccer stadium** in the Bronx, a **Coney Island amphitheater** and a **residential complex** at the former Domino sugar factory in Brooklyn, could still be halted or changed. The Domino project has won widespread support, but Mr. de Blasio has expressed "serious concerns" about a **proposed $350 million soccer stadium near Yankee Stadium** because the Bloomberg administration planned to provide **the soccer team's wealthy owners with public resources, including tax exemptions.** (Bagli, 2013 – emphasis added)

And that's another aspect of the developer's grotesque greed: tax breaks and tax incentives that are offered to builders. Along with this comes the blatant abuse of what is called Tax Increment Financing, a way to lie about the wealth of an area and then beg for tax assistance promising to improve it. It is far more complex, but the point to be made is that these white men continually abuse it.

But in addition to that are the rich white boys who can afford to put the cart before the horse. There is already a stadium or a basketball arena or a football complex? Who gives a shit. They want a bigger and better one so they can attract more fans and patrons and make more money. So they lay out the plans, look for a giant corporation whose name they can plaster on it in exchange for tens or hundreds of millions of dollars for a decade long deal, and it's done.

Here are some examples: Toyota Center (Houston, NFL), American Airlines Center (Dallas, NBA), Bank of America Stadium (Charlotte, NFL), FedEx Field (Landover, Maryland – NFL), Philips Areana (Atlanta, NBA), Mercedes-Benz Superdome (New Orleans, NFL) and another one Mercedes-Benz Stadium in Atlanta, Levi's Stadium (Santa Clara, CA – NFL) and AT&T Stadium (Dallas – NFL). And this is just the tip of the iceberg.

Wealthy owners get the stadiums built using tax incentives and with the help of mayors and developers. This huge revenue stream, once built, means decades of income for these white boys who then have the nerve to complain about player salaries and the like. The revenue from those ticket sales help pay for that structure and those salaries. Once again, the developers and contractors make out like fat rats and the public just applauds and goes out and buys fan merchandise – which of course the owners also get a piece of.

Continuing:

> The Bloomberg administration has also **granted tax breaks worth tens of millions of dollars** for the first phase of the $3 billion Willets Point project in Queens, for a proposed **office tower** on the West Side of Manhattan and for the **outlet mall** on Staten Island. **"They made no secret about the fact that they're working very hard to lock in a number of major projects for the future,"** said Brad Lander, a councilman from Brooklyn. "De Blasio said everything will be reviewed.

But some things can be reviewed and changed more than others." (Bagli, 2013)

What is not mentioned is that each of the boroughs where construction will take place has representatives who also get a piece of the pie – usually under the table. So these white men, like the Galveston trio that created the Commission concept back in the late 1800s, get together with their fellow millionaire and billionaire friends, and work like hell to alter skylines and create structures that will generate revenue.

When Bloomberg left, in came Bill de Blasio, whose claim to fame was that he was married to a black woman.

> For his part, Mr. de Blasio, who was the city's public advocate before being elected mayor, opposed few projects during the Bloomberg era and embraced the notion of high-density development near transit centers. But he has made it clear that he will drive a harder bargain with developers to get the best deal for taxpayers. During his mayoral campaign, Mr. de Blasio also vowed "wholesale reform of our city's tax incentive policies that give hundreds of millions of dollars to office towers on Park Avenue and unaccountable one-shot subsidies to companies who can do without them." (Bagli, 2013)

De Blasio is an interesting person for a number of reasons. According to one background piece on de Blasio,

> A self-identified populist, de Blasio has expressed concern with the stark level of economic inequality in New York City, which he has called the "tale of two cities". He has publicly supported a socially liberal, progressive, and neoliberal discourse on the city's economy, urban planning, public education, police relations, and privatization. De Blasio has maintained high approval rates and levels of public support throughout his tenure, albeit slightly lower than his predecessor, Michael Bloomberg.(Wikipedia, 2018)

Let's hold it here for a minute. We know that New York is a city full of Jews, Irish, and a number of other white ethnics whose ancestors came over here from somewhere seeking a better life. The Statue of Liberty, sitting out in New York Harbor, reads,

> Not like the brazen giant of Greek fame,
> With conquering limbs astride from land to land;
> Here at our sea-washed, sunset gates shall stand
> A mighty woman with a torch, whose flame

> Is the imprisoned lightning, and her name
> Mother of Exiles. From her beacon-hand
> Glows world-wide welcome; her mild eyes command
> The air-bridged harbor that twin cities frame.
> "Keep, ancient lands, your storied pomp!" cries she
> With silent lips. **"Give me your tired, your poor,**
> **Your huddled masses yearning to breathe free,**
> The wretched refuse of your teeming shore.
> Send these, the homeless, tempest-tossed to me,
> I lift my lamp beside the golden door!" (emphasis added)

One last point before we move on with New York's mayors, developers and their love of statues, buildings, towers and such. The beautiful words you just read were on the statue which was officially unveiled on October 20, 1886. As you may remember, African people in America were enslaved in the southern part of this country and considered the "property" of whites. This division exists in every decision that a white man with power makes when he is designing his city: that is, how do we show white supremacy without pissing off the niggers? More on this later.

In New York, anyone running for office therefore has to court Jewish support. That means changing one's name if it is necessary, and it means throwing shade on the opposition if need be. Both took place during de Blasio's campaign. In an article titled, "Dietl Questions de Blasioi's Name and Heart," Azi Paybarah of *Politico* shared the following:

> Independent mayoral candidate Bo Dietl on Monday, in the course of being endorsed for mayor by a Republican City Council member, accused Mayor Bill de Blasio of **changing his name in a cynical ploy to court Jewish voters and of potentially lacking a heart**. "He's very cold. He's very calculating," Dietl said of de Blasio, outside City Hall with Queens Councilman Eric Ulrich by his side. (Paybarah, 2017 – emphasis added)

This kind f mud-slinging takes place all over America and much of it has to do with race, from the Deep South to California, these white people don't miss a beat. It's all about power and if you can't deal with the racial issue, you might be considered "soft." Jews are not a "race," but they are a controversial group because of their history elsewhere in the world. At any rate, back to the Dietl and de Blasio race:

> When a reporter asked Dietl about an anti-Semitic City Council candidate running in Upper Manhattan, Dietl said, "Anyone who uses any anti-Semitic tones, I'm against." **Noting his ex-wife, children and**

> **grandchildren are Jewish,** he added, **"I've got Jewish in me."** Then,
> turning his focus to de Blasio, Dietl added, "Hmm. What was his real
> name? Warren Wilhelm? Why did he change it? My first question at my
> first debate: Why did you change your name from Warren Wilhelm? I'm
> Dietl, Bo Dietl. Warren Wilhelm, did he change it? That's a good
> question (Paybarah, 2017 – emphasis added).

How is this white boy "carrying Jewish in me," and exactly how is that done? The big city bids for mayor will eventually touch on issues of race and ethnicity and much of the argument is as ludicrous as the one you just read. Be that as it may, the changing of the name is nothing new. Jews (and Italians) have been changing their names every since they arrived in this country. This is especially true of the ones that were seeking celebrity in some capacity.

For instance, Tony Curtis (Bernie Schwartz), Lorene Greene (Chaim Leibowiz), Rodney Dangerfield (Jacob Cohen), Jon Stewart (Jonathan Stuart Leibowitz), Larry King (Larry Zeigler), Natalie Portman (Natalie Hershlag), George Burns (Nathan Birnbaum), Gene Wilder (Jerome Silberman), Jerry Lewis (Joseph Levitch), and so many more. Most of them in Hollywood making it famous using their "altered" names.

Back to the New York race, Jews and the name-changing. Dietz further explicates,

> I want my Jewish friends to think — and you saw how he came against
> Israel. He came against Israel. I support Israel. He doesn't support Israel.
> When told of Dietl's comments, de Blasio campaign spokesman Dan
> Levitan said in a statement, "Bill de Blasio is a strong supporter of Israel
> and any suggestion otherwise is silly and offensive." (Paybarah, 2017)

Israel. That is how you test your "Jewishness." In elections all over the country you hear them talking about how often the "visit" Israel and who they are related to. De Blasio's name change can be explained, thusly:

> De Blasio was born Warren Wilhelm, Jr., named after his father. In
> 1983, after graduating New York University, **he took his mother's
> maiden name, de Blasio,** having become estranged from his father.
> Over the years, he began calling himself William, instead of Warren,
> **and formally changed his name ahead of his 2001 race for City
> Council**. (Paybarah, 2017 – emphasis added)

So the fact is that De Blasio was hiding something. But I added the background information to show you, the reader, that this is nothing new. When I lived in Chicago from 1986-1987, Jewish men would marry Latino women and then change their last name to HER surname so it appeared as if any "hires" that were made were minority! This went on under the Washington Administration, a black man who had more than his problem with Jewish opposition.

Continuing with the name change information:

> When asked why he thought de Blasio changed his name, Dietl replied, "Because I think he wanted to run for mayor of New York and not have the idea that he was German." When asked why he thought not having a German name was preferable to voters, Dietl replied, "Because he might have a negative Jewish vote against him. That's my feeling. Why would you change your name? Aren't you proud of your name? I'm proud of my name. I don't want to change it." (Paybarah, 2017)

Dietl nevertheless got his ass kicked in the election and De Blasio became Mayor.

But black to Bloomberg:

> **Real estate developers and investors, who had a familiar ally in Mr. Bloomberg, will be watching for early signs of Mr. de Blasio's agenda**. A spokeswoman for Mr. de Blasio, Lis Smith, said he would "review every project with an eye toward maximizing affordable housing, good jobs and value for taxpayers." (Bagli, 2013)

Recall the first line about how those developers and investors would "be watching for early signs of Mr. de Blasio's agenda." In other words, they want to see if he is going to bend to the rules that were set by his predecessor, Michael Bloomberg. This is how it works. The previous mayor has paid off and solicited the support of all these major developers and if that mayor loses or it not re-elected, then those developers are on to the next person to test his/her allegiance to the developer's projects.

For instance, when looking back at the Bloomberg administration, the developers found,

> Only one so-called legacy project — the rezoning of 73 blocks surrounding Grand Central Terminal for taller towers — failed, when the Bloomberg administration could not win the Council's support last month. (Bagli, 2013)

Can you see how tenuous one's "legacy" can be when placed in the hands of another? According to the Bagli article, "Many projects are rooted in the early days of Mr. Bloomberg's 12-year tenure and were steered by his first deputy mayor and chief development architect, Daniel L. Doctoroff. More than once, Mr. Bloomberg has said that Mr. Doctoroff, and by extension himself, had a "greater impact on this city, I think, than Robert Moses." (Bagli, 2013)

Bloomberg should watch his words. Robert Moses, for you who don't know, is one of the most profound and impactful and was known as a "master builder." It was also clear that he was a racist, which goes back to my earlier points about the inevitable link between urban and land decisions and how these white men who make these decisions view people of color.

One source informs us,

> Known as the "master builder" of mid-20th century New York City, Long Island, Rockland County, and Westchester County, he is sometimes compared to Baron Haussmann of Second EmpireParis, and was one of the most polarizing figures in the history of urban development in the United States. His decisions favoring highways over public transit helped create the modern suburbs of Long Island and influenced a generation of engineers, architects, and urban planners who spread his philosophies across the nation despite his not having trained in those professions (Wikipedia, 2018)

And remember what I wrote earlier about race the impact is has on the attitudes of decision makers, including planners, developers and mayors? Well check out the following:

> Moses vocally opposed allowing black war veterans to move into Stuyvesant Town, a Manhattan residential development complex created to house World War II veterans … In response to the biography, **Moses defended his forced displacement of poor and minority communities as an inevitable part of urban revitalization**, stating "I **raise my stein to the builder who can remove ghettos without moving people as I hail the chef who can make omelets without breaking eggs**" … Additionally, close associates of Moses claimed that they could keep African Americans from using pools in neighborhoods with predominantly white populations **by making the water too cold.** (Wikipedia, 2018 – emphasis added)

This is a man who has gone down in history as a "master planner." And you see what he thinks about people of color. That is par for the course. I'm trying to tell you that these white boys don't get "less racist" because the go up in the ranks or receive a promotion, a credential or an award. They become MORE racist because the white cultural super ego is dependent on the subjugation of those who are not white and those who are poor! History proves this and their own "experts" and "Master planners" clearly show what they think in their writings and statements. But in the urban planning classes around America, the instructors won't mention Moses' racist views. And if a black student brings it up, his sources are questioned.

That is, unless that student is ME. I come loaded for bear. I study not only Moses, but the people that HE studied under. I don't just look at his statements about the ghetto, but also about other actions he took, the meetings he spoke at, the testimonies he gave. And then after that I put together a book of knowledge, akin to this one, that strips people like Moses of his undeserved reputation, a book that also includes exposing the instructors who use Moses as a reference point. Oppression is collective and therefore so should be our opposition to it. If the son thinks that way, he learned it from his daddy. So his daddy gets an ass kicking as well.

Back to the issue of Mayors Bloomberg and De Blasio and the role of developers in the on-going land speculation and massive construction projects taking place in the Big Apple. The article makes the claim that, "New York mayors have traditionally rushed through favored projects in the closing days of their administrations, and rarely has a new mayor upended his predecessor's work" (Bagli, 2013). That statement is most likely bullshit, but I simply don't have the time to do a longitudinal assessment of the mayors of New York.

But there are some basic facts that we can deduce from the actions of both Bloomberg and De Blasio.

One is the emphasis on the high rise office building. That has little, if anything, to do with people of color. A second is the focus on malls and various types of recreational stadiums. A third is the waterfront development and the high prices of the goods and services offered and the fact that only some New Yorkers will be able to afford to participate in these riverfront/waterfront activities.

Going back before Bloomberg we had Mayor Giuliani. According to the article,

> Before leaving office in 2001, Mayor Rudolph W. Giuliani **signed a secret deal to build new stadiums for the city's two professional baseball teams, the Yankees and the Mets**. Less than a month later, Mayor Bloomberg effectively scuttled the agreement, citing the city's more pressing civic needs after the terrorist attack on the World Trade Center. **But the Yankees and the Mets did get new stadiums, replete with city subsidies worth tens of millions of dollars**. (Bagli, 2013 – emphasis added)

How does the writer know that there was a "secret deal" if it was a secret? If two stadiums were going to be built, how could that possibly be kept secret? Those stadiums represented revenue streams and weren't about to be passed up or abandoned and as the excerpt makes plain, they were eventually built. White people need that sports outlet because so few of them are any good at it. They go to games to see blacks and Latinos perform. We score all the touchdowns, we gain all the yards, we make the great catches and get on base and we are the ones who can dunk backwards. This is the fact of the matter. It's like a trip to the zoo, only the "animals" that are being "observed" are human.

Back to Giuliani:

> **Mr. Giuliani himself railed for years about Mayor David N. Dinkins's last-minute deal to build a new stadium at the National Tennis Center in Queens.** But he did nothing to stop the project, other than bar his senior officials from attending the U.S. Open there. (Bagli, 2013 = emphasis added)

"Railed for years." Just like a jealous, scatter-brained old bitch.

Again, we see the white politician attacking the black politician for no reason other than the attack itself. What Giuliani did is the same thing that Trump did to Obama. These white men have racial issues that they cannot address so their first step is denial and then transference. That was in 1997 and the Tennis Center was named after Arthur Ashe. The white man, jealous that a black man had defeated him for Mayor, continues to act like a spoiled brat, just as Trump is now doing over Obama's legacy, and the evidence follows:

> The officials said that the Mayor had a longstanding invitation to make a speech to inaugurate the Arthur Ashe Stadium on Monday night. They noted that he would be speaking before a national television audience and that they had provided him with a draft of a short, gracious speech about the late Mr. Ashe and the sporting event … But tennis officials expressed concern that the Mayor's lack of response was linked to a political battle **that goes back to the 1993 mayoral race between New York's No. 1 Yankee fan and New York's No. 1 tennis aficionado, David N. Dinkins.** (Krause, 1997 – emphasis added)

Giuliani was jealous, but got payback later in the next election when he defeated Dinkins. But the fact still remains that,

> **It was Mayor Dinkins who negotiated the deal with the U.S.T.A. that made the new 23,000-seat sadium possible and that will keep the tournament in Flushing Meadows, Queens, for at least 25 more years.** Under the contract, the association was given 21 acres of parkland, doubling the size of the National Tennis Center, and the expansion and new stadium were paid for by the tennis association with financing through tax-exempt Industrial Development Agency bonds. (Krause, 1997 – emphasis added)

The black man does the work and the white man tries to take the credit – just like Trump continues to try to do with his lies regarding Obama. And that is why today, some two decades later, Trump turns to Giuliani to work with the case because, like Trump, Giulianis is a spineless, lying piece of shit.

And now I conclude having shared with you the escapes of four (4) New York mayors: Giuliani, Dinkins, Bloomberg and finally, De Blasio. This political primer has been most instructive. As we walked into De Blasio's recent election (he has now been in office five years), take note of the role of developers and "others":

> **The City Planning Department has certified for public review a $1.5 billion plan** by Two Trees Management to transform the former Domino Sugar mill on the East River into an 11-acre residential complex with office space, a park and 2,100 apartments, 660 for moderate- and middle-income tenants. There may be some additional bargaining **over concessions from the developer before the Council votes on the project** … Mr. de Blasio, **who has named only a few of his top officials**, has yet to announce **who will serve as his administration's point person on economic development**. (Bagli, 2013 – emphasis added)

The City Planning Department. Perhaps the setup is differently in New York than it is in a city the size of Omaha, because in the latter context those planners couldn't certify a pig to eat slop. They are just rubber stamps, some with credentials and some without. They do the bidding of the local "consultants" who are themselves former directors of the very same planning department. If not that, then some major developer or contract – Peter Kiewit and Sons, Hawkins Construction, Wietz Construction or any of the others – get the call for "a meeting" where they can begin discussing the "plans" that they feel will make Omaha more of a tourism attraction than what it has been for the past half century: the largest city in what most people recognized as a "flyover state."

Take note the naming of a "point person on economic development." This is not going to be a person of color because when these white men think about development they think about benefits to and for the white race, the people with the money – the people who VOTE. The point person is going to be someone who can plan and map out structures and projects that are going to generate revenue streams that can expand and enhance the future of the city.

This just in – we'll call it "the case of the secret file addendum."

On September 21, 2018 it was reported in the New York Daily News that Mayor De Blasio had been keeping some secret files. Following is that story and my relevant response to it:

> Lease for new city Department of Investigation headquarters at 180 Maiden Lane **will cost taxpayers $352.7 million over 20 years**. City

> Controller Scott Stringer on Friday questioned the city's efforts to push through a huge $352 million, 20-year lease for the city Department of Investigation's new office space three blocks away from its current location. (Smith, 2018 – emphasis added)

And why didn't the administrators know about that expensive idea before? The previous mayor kept it a secret, that's why:

> The lease was at the heart of **a secret dossier**, first revealed by the Daily News, **that Mayor de Blasio kept on DOI Commissioner Mark Peters** documenting allegations of threats and abusive behavior. (Smith, 2018) In July, Stringer questioned the excessive costs of the real estate deal and refused to approve the lease. A month later, the Department of Citywide Administrative Services (DCAS) went ahead and registered the lease anyway. "This situation is deeply concerning," Stringer said. **"After the Rivington scandal, the city promised New Yorkers it would strive to make fiscally responsible real estate decisions, and to do so in a more transparent way. This feels like deja vu all over again."** (Smith, 2018 – emphasis added)

White men acting like children and playing games with hundreds of millions of other people's money. But this was not the first time – some brief history is in line before we continue with the current scandal:

> **Three years ago**, Bill de Blasio was the little-known mayoral candidate who wouldn't budge. Police wanted him and several other protesters to clear away from the front of the State University of New York's midtown headquarters. De Blasio — the audacious leader, standing his ground, **preventing SUNY from closing Long Island College Hospital and converting it to luxury condos** — was handcuffed. He was out of jail a few hours later. (Barkan, 2016)

So a university wanted to convert a closed hospital to luxury condos – for what? Profit? Of course. Again we see the true motives of the white man's institutions, even higher education. It's always about the money. De Blasio, who was and remains super-rich, put on a grandstand play, got arrested and that move won him a place in City Hall. But there were more land-related scandals:

> That theatrical act of civil disobedience helped catapult de Blasio to City Hall. **But now the progressive Democrat is drowning in scandals**. At least one of those is probably just political ax-grinding: The dubious fundraising for state senate candidates is likely defensible in the end. And the alleged quid pro quo revolving around de Blasio's haphazard attempts to ban horse-drawn carriages was more peculiar than insidious. But if there's an Achilles' heel here that could cripple the mayor, **it's**

> **Rivington House — the unseemly land deal that may…turn a
> healthcare facility into luxury condos.** (Barkan, 2016 – emphasis
> added)

Now we come to the Rivingon scandal and the developers and the land
question. It's all about flipping property:

> The basic facts of the Rivington deal **reek of old machine politics**: In
> the course of several months, Village Care, **which operated the hospice
> for AIDS patients on the Lower East Side, was permitted to sell the
> building for $28 million to the Allure Group, a for-profit healthcare
> provider.** That low price was a function of the fact that a deed restriction
> dating back to 1992 required that the block-long property remain a
> nonprofit residential healthcare facility in perpetuity. **Once the sale was
> complete, however, Allure paid $16 million to the city to lift the deed
> restriction and proceeded to flip the Rivington building to Slate
> Property Group, a condominium developer, for $116 million.**
> (Barkan, 2016 – emphasis added)

This is the scandal that De Blasio was able to get out of. He enabled one
corporation to flip a property and make more than $100 million in doing so. Again
as the article says, "old machine politics." Land, profit, a condominium developer
– and a mayor.

Stringer well remembered what De Blasio had done. So now we come fast
forward to and as a result,

> Stringer was highly critical of DCAS last year over its **bungling of a
> waiver that allowed** the owners of a nursing home on Rivington St. in
> the Lower East Side to sell the property to **a luxury condo developer**,
> contrary to the deed's requirement that the building remain a facility for
> the elderly or infirm. **"Here again we have a real estate deal that
> involves hundreds of millions of dollars, and here again DCAS is
> refusing to answer even basic questions,"** Stringer said. "DCAS should
> suspend work until all questions are answered about this significant
> project." (Smith, 2018)

Luxury condos. This has nothing to do with the minority population or poor
people. This is white men playing beach blanket bingo with hundreds of millions
of dollars and using political power to do so. They run for office and then make
money working with developers and planners to dominate and direct what the city
will look like. But in doing this, they also control who will be put to work on the
project, who will be employed once the project is complete and how the project
will impact the community that it is located in.

> The lease, which would consolidate DOI offices into one space inside a sleek glass building overlooking the East River, **is one of the most expensive city rentals**. Along with the monthly rent, **the city is footing most of the costs of an extensive renovation: Taxpayers will fund $35 million out of the planned $43 million overhaul.** But in a letter to DCAS Commissioner Lisette Camillo sent Friday, Deputy Controller Lisa Flores noted that DOI's current lease doesn't expire for seven years and **the estimated cost of the new lease does not factor in operating expenses and property tax payments that the landlord passes on to the tenant**. (Smith, 2018 – emphasis added)

In the words of Silky Slim (Calvin Lockhart) from the 1974 movie "Uptown Saturday Night," 'never have so few benefitted so much from so many.' And that is what is going on with this Rivington deal. Once again we have a "luxury condo developer" involved with the mayor of the city. But this time the long term pain for the taxpayer could bear the brunt of the cost, not to mention the real-life potential of future rents at the location being employed to assist with those costs.

So because of all this, behind-the-scenes dickering took place and De Blasio came up with a "secret dossier":

> … In May of last year, Camillo promised to cut costs by making sure if one city agency leaves a space, another will take over so that taxpayers aren't paying to for empty space. The DOI plan had no such plan for a replacement tenant at the agency's current location at 80 Maiden Lane. **As revealed by The News, a secret dossier assembled by City Hall to give de Blasio reasons to fire DOI head Peters included three incidents of Peters allegedly making abusive and threatening comments as he fought with DCAS over the new office lease**. Peters denied making threats but admitted that the process of negotiating the new office space with DCAS was "tense." (Smith, 2018 – emphasis added)

New York, New York.

We have an idea of the politics behind the development in the largest city in America and the 10th largest in the world with a population f 18,604,000. Now let's go to the second largest city in America: Los Angeles.

Los Angeles Mayor Rick Caruso and the Developers

This article is about the power and impact of a major developer – mall developer, specifically – and his impact on City Hall.

In 2016 Rick Caruso was looking for approval for a 240-foot luxury tower next to the Beverly Center, promoted as L.A.'s "premiere "food, fashion and shopping destination."

The article states:

> Retail impresario Rick Caruso has already made his mark on the Los Angeles landscape with shopping wonderlands like The Grove and The Americana, but now the developer is looking upward. (Wattenhofer, 2016)

According to Crusoe's website, his next plan is as follows:

> Caruso's latest project is 333 La Cienega, a 20-story luxury residential tower that would alter the skyline in Beverly Grove (13 of the 145 residential units would be earmarked for tenants earning very low and moderate incomes). The 240-foot tower would soar well above the neighborhood's height restriction of 45 feet, requiring a zoning change from the city planning department. (Wattenhofer, 2016)

Caruso's website is even more descriptive and ambitious:

> Expected to open in 2020, 333 La Cienega will offer 145 state-of-the-art units for rent, 10% of which will be designated affordable housing. The project also includes a wide array of community benefits that will transform the outdated Loehmann's site into a central gathering place for residents, neighbors and visitors to enhance the entire neighborhood. 333 La Cienega is located at the gateway between Los Angeles and Beverly Hills at the intersection of Burton Way, La Cienega and San Vicente Boulevards, less than a half-mile from the new Purple Line subway stop. (Caruso, 2018)

With the plans all but boasted about – but not yet built – the bombast and braggadocio serve as the "lure", the "source" for the greasing of palms and the leeching for donations. As Wattenhofer (2016) writes,

> As the La Cienega tower moves to City Hall for final approval, the *Los Angeles Times* reports that, **over the past five years, Caruso and his family members and employees have contributed about $470,000 to local politicians and their pet projects.** Among them, a $125,000 donation to the Mayor's Fund **at the request of Mayor Eric Garcetti**, a $200,000 contribution supporting the Measure M campaign, and **$100,000 to Councilman** Mike Bonin's Los Angeles Forward project. (Wattenhofer, 2016 – emphasis added)

And this is the process. In smaller cities you may not hear much about these kinds of payments because the local newspapers have historically been controlled by City Hall, ever since the days of the penny press. In Omaha, the largest newspaper in the state controls every other newspaper in the entire state but a few, and it is nothing more than a mouthpiece for City Hall, the county board, the state and all things Nebraska and conservative. Therefore a repeat of the same types of "political wheeling and dealing" can continue, unabated, and the staid atmosphere of a hick town that is working to sound as if it is a "metro" or if it is "urbane," remains in place.

As for Los Angeles, the politics move hot and heavy as Wattenhofer writes, "For Caruso, **donations have proven effective when dealing with disgruntled neighbors.** (Wattenhofer, 2016 – emphasis added). By "neighbors" the article is referring to nearby business neighbors who may be put aback by the coming of another mega-mall in the area. Even the ones inside of the Beverly Center may feel a little intimidated – nothing that a little bribe money can't cure.

One such "problem" is described below:

> According to the *Times*, several residents of 333 La Cienega's neighbor, the Westbury Terrace condo building, petitioned the neighborhood council about the La Cienega project, **worried the Caruso tower would block their views and increase traffic in the surrounding area.** But after Caruso **agreed to make $500,000 in improvements to the Westbury Terrace building,** many of those petitioners spoke out in favor of the La Cienega tower. (Wattenhofer, 2016 – emphasis added)

And this is all it takes in many instances. These power brokers go back and forth and manipulate the geography of downtowns and prepare them for the kind of people that THEY want to see walking the pedestrial walkways and cruising along the boulevard. They want to see a certain "type" on the escalators and getting into the elevators. This is the big city political developer and speculators at work. People like Caruso call it cooperation or negotiating; I call it racist interlocking directorates at work. Put another way,

> Caruso himself seems to view his financial actions as simply **making the necessary concessions to his detractors in order to move forward**. As he tells the *Times*, "The way I get the community to support the project is to give them what they want. (Wattenhofer, 2016)

And when you have the kind of money and capital that Caruso undoubtedly has, you can afford to have a philosophy like this. It sounds like an act of sincere benevolence when, in reality, it is crony capitalism in its purest form.

Los Angeles Ethics Commission and the Developers

Long after Caruso got his mega mall started, there was a concern raised by the Los Angeles Ethnics Commission regarding proposed bans on developer donations. I include this story from the *Los Angeles Times* of August 21, 2018 only because it offers some attempt at "balance" by the powers that be when, in reality, the concept of "ethics" is in and of itself a façade.

Let the teaching moment begin:

> **The Los Angeles City Ethics Commission** tabled **a proposal to ban political donations from real estate developers on Tuesday**, citing legal and practical concerns with the idea. Commissioners did not vote down the proposal but **deferred a decision on it**, saying they wanted to look more closely at who would be covered by such restrictions. For example, commission staff cautioned that **a person who seeks council approval for a new development may not be the one whose financial interests are at stake.** (Reyes & Zahniser, 2018 – emphasis added).

Deferred a decision on a proposal to ban political donations from real estate developers. The reason is that a person who seeks council approval for a new development may not be the one whose financial interests are at stake. This is bullshit. The person making the presentations is a duly noted "representative" of the project and is therefore someone whose personal and social interests are at stake. Locating the financial source is just a case of "following the money."

That deferment is a stall tactic and the reason given is superficial, at best. But this is what they do: it is the APPEARANCE of ethics, akin to Omaha, Nebraska's so called Ethics Alliance, that is of importance. I analyzed over 200 member businesses of this alliance and sent a copy of my conclusions, charging them with being hypocrites since their collective existence took place when racial segregation was the rule, and despite their "ethics" they did nothing. There was not a single response.

In the case of Los Angeles and the "deferred decision,"

> The move means that a ban will not be in place when fundraising starts next month for the **2020 municipal election, which will involve seven open City Council seats** — two of them vacant due to term limits. **City rules allow candidates in those races to raise money for a year and a half leading up to a primary election**. (Reyes & Zahniser, 2018 – emphasis added).

These people go through all the motions to present a "united front" in terms of their façade. Ethics? In politics? Are you serious? Morality, when it comes to government, is relative and situational. Everyone knows it just as the jokes about lawyers being crooked is a backhanded way of stating that the profession is filled with crooks. Ethics Commission? Made up of whom? Unethical people.

Moving on:

> Commissioners said they were willing to explore an alternative proposal: **requiring elected officials to recuse themselves from decisions on a development proposal if they had received a donation from the developer** who involved in the project. (Reyes & Zahniser, 2018 – emphasis added).

What was just proposed as an "alternative" should have been the primary proposal under consideration. If recused, then those getting money cannot favor one project over another. That solves the problem. But that is too much of an "ethical" approach and these people don't really want to make any changes in campaign finance. The people making the donations want to see, first hand, where their donations are going and how hard the people they gave the money to are fighting for them:

> That idea was raised by Los Angeles City Councilman David Ryu, **who has spent the past three years pushing for new restrictions on donations at City Hall.** Ryu and four of his colleagues proposed a ban on campaign contributions from developers whose building projects were up for city approval, saying it would counter the perception that money drives city decisions about what gets built. (Reyes & Zahniser, 2018 – emphasis added).

Now the members on the council who are serious about real reform have been identified and will be treated accordingly. No donations from realtors and perhaps a slander campaign or two as well. These greedy developers are serious and they won't allow anyone to stand in their way, right and wrong be damned!

In any case, resistance was on the way:

> Their proposal was rolled out in January 2017, just as city leaders were gearing up to fight Measure S, which would have imposed new restrictions on real estate **projects that cannot be approved without changing city planning rules.** After the ballot measure was handily defeated, the proposed ban failed to move forward at City Hall. (Reyes & Zahniser, 2018).

And this is where that "interlocking directorate" of planners, developers, land speculators and others comes into play. The ballot measure failed because the council was messing with rich people's money, and that cannot be allowed. When it's the poor, the minority or the otherwise disenfranchised, that's one thing: but white men are not going to allow anyone to impact upon the money that is used to pay the mortgage on their gated community condos or their family vans for their wives. It's going on all over the country folks, and I'm just trying to let you know that these actions are being pawned off as "business as usual" and nobody's doing a god damn thing about it!

The developers have people speaking up for them, not matter how shall their arguments are. For instance, note the following:

> At Tuesday's meeting, **Commission President** Serena Oberstein said she feared that banning developers from giving such donations **would only encourage them to pour money into independent expenditure committees, which face no limits on the size of donations**. Oberstein also questioned **whether there was "concrete proof" that campaign money from developers leads to corruption at City Hall.** And she cited concerns from Ethics Commission staffers, who had warned that **figuring out who should be targeted by such a ban would be complicated.** (Reyes & Zahniser, 2018 – emphasis added).

This woman doesn't know her ass from a hole in the ground – at least that is the way she sounds. The money is going to get to the right people no matter how much legislation is passed. Some will get caught, others will not. But when a women like Oberstein doubts if there is any "concrete proof" that campaign money from developers leads to corruption at City Hall, she is going against every single scholarly and relevant investigation ever conducted by political scientists. And one need not be a political scientist to have read the Machiavellian contention that "power corrupts and absolute power corrupts absolutely." And what is the greatest corruptor in politics? Money.

Figuring out who should be targeted would be complicated, she adds? Is this woman smoking crack or what? The people who should be targeted are the ones with the most money to give at present and the ones who have given in the past. All you have to do is "follow the money," which is easy enough to do since all campaign contributions have to be reported. If reports are falsified, then that means the "target" should include the donor and the folks who keep the records. It's very simple but to claim that it's complicated is this woman's way of bamboozling the weak-minded public into thinking that the council really gives a damn.

One member of that council does, it seems:

> Ryu had sought to answer that question: In a memo prepared for the councilman and his staffers, **attorney Stephen Kaufman suggested that such restrictions could specifically target individuals or companies and their principals applying for city approval for large**

development projects. However, commission staffers pointed out in a report that the person who seeks city approval for a project **may be the property owner, architect, lobbyist or someone else.** (Reyes & Zahniser, 2018 – emphasis added).

That may be true, but these people have to get paid by somebody for their actions, either by check or cash. And that cash has to exchange hands at some point in time. And that is where "following the money" and whoever is handling it, comes in handy. White people are clumsy and when they think they are being the slickest and the coolest, that's when they're at their clumsiest. Remember the Watergate break-in? The property owner, the architect or the lobbyist still have to handle money at some point, and that is the key to the colors. I agree with Commissioner Ryu: target individuals or companies and their principals applying for city approval for large development projects. Greed begets more greed and the more successful these principals have been in the past, the more lax they will be in the future. That is how you nail them.

Moving right along:

> Commissioner Andrea Sheridan Ordin said that with an election coming up quickly, **"this is not the answer," but "there ought to be an answer."** Coalition to Preserve L.A. spokeswoman Ileana Wachtel, whose group backed Measure S and **has repeatedly raised concerns about the influence of real estate interests,** said the recusal idea was worthwhile. Still, she called it a "cop out" to say it is too hard to figure out who should fall under a developer donation ban. "It certainly seems like this body of educated, smart people could figure out some kind of definition," Wachtel said. (Reyes & Zahniser, 2018 – emphasis added).

Those people are elected by lazy people who expect them to have all the answers. But when the answer impacts on who gets paid or not, that is the time when, as Commissioner Ordin claimed, "there ought to be an answer." In fact, you have to keep an eye on those Commissioners as well; they may be taking some under the table money, especially when a proposed project is in their district. In small-time Omaha, for instance, it is not uncommon for Commissioners and Council members alike to "flip flop overnight" on a construction project. That means somebody got to them. And nobody is the wiser. Such actions take place all over the country and in every case, guess who benefits? The mayors and the developers.

Cincinnati's Mayor's Race and Developers

Next we come to Cincinnati, Ohio – the so-called "heartland." But the heart of a monster is the most important part, and American political and urban corruption has a long history. Therefore its component parts are also more than likely involved.

One source informs us that, "With a population of 301,301, Cincinnati is the third-largest city in Ohio and 65th in the United States. It is the fastest growing economic power in the Midwestern United States. Based on percentages … and the 28th-biggest metropolitan statistical area in the U.S. Cincinnati is also within a single day's drive of two-thirds of the United States populace.(Coolidge, 2017). What does this tell us?

It says that the person vying to be mayor of this city realizes that they are going to have a lot of "juice." They have a professional sport team in both baseball and football, and they have access to a riverfront. And that is when the donors come out, big time.

An article titled, "Biggest Donors to John Cranley, Yvette Simpson in Cincinnati Mayor Race? Developers." That headline says it all, doesn't it. These developers see dollar signs in a city that is continuing to build and expand its downtown, its economic base and its personality.

Cranley won the election (white male) over Simpson (a black woman) and it should be noted that he did better than expected in the black areas and really cleaned up in the conservative sections of town. What else is new? At any rate, he claimed that his three priorities were going to be the sewers, something called a housing counselor and public transportation. With the exception of the counselor, the others involve bids from developers.

The focus of this section is the mayor's race itself and the role that developers played. According to Pilcher & Wirt (2017),

> **Real estate developers have spent more money than any other sector in the Cincinnati mayor's race,** according to an exclusive Enquirer analysis of campaign contributions to incumbent John Cranley and challenger Yvette Simpson. **Developers gave much more to Cranley's campaign,** the analysis shows, **but their donations also accounted for the largest share of Simpson's total at more than 10 percent.** (Pilcher & Wert, 2017 – emphasis added)

Again, notice the role of race: the developers back the white man with a pittance going to the black female. Coincidence? Hardly not. Cincinnati has a racist tradition and several riots in recent years clearly show this to be the case. Note where the developers donated more than any other sector, which means that they know the importance of the mayor and they are already chomping at the bit to get their plans and land speculations on the desk of the mayor and whoever he or she will appoint to make the planning decisions.

And note this and the issue of campaign contributions. According to the Cincinnati Enquirer newspaper, "The finding was one of several to come from a searchable database created by The Enquirer to provide better public access to the campaign contributions made to both Cranley and his challenger, fellow Democrat and Councilwoman Simpson. **It comes at a time when city support for development projects is being questioned and the contribution levels of some business leaders – including developers – are the subject of a lawsuit**" (Pilcher & Wert, 2017 – emphasis added)

I was not able to home in on the specifics of the lawsuit, but after Cranley won the election, the following was brought to the fore:

> Three-and-a-half months before the city of Cincinnati settled any outstanding claims with former City Manager Harry Black, Black's attorney wrote the city solicitor a letter accusing Mayor John Cranley of violating the city's charter by interfering in personnel matters **and economic development and giving developers "sweetheart" deals that contributed to the city's deficit**. (Wetterich, 2018 – emphasis added).

"Sweetheart deals." And note that developers contributed most heavily to his campaign. Quid pro quo. The mayor chooses who the city manager will be, and that is how the palms get greased. More on this later. During the election,

> Here are some of The Enquirer's key findings: The two campaigns are using dramatically different strategies for fundraising. Simpson is getting a lot of smaller donations from a lot more people, especially online. Meanwhile, Cranley got bigger contributions from a smaller set of donors. The Enquirer found one Cranley donor who is under indictment, prompting the campaign to redirect that donation to a charity. (Pilcher & Wert, 2017).

Bigger contributions from a smaller set of donors – translation: rich white folks and those "developers" we talked about. Not only that, but "Donations from separate companies owned by the same person grew this campaign season, creating controversy around the practice" (Pilcher & Wert, 2017).

What is clear is that the developers played a monumental role in Cranley's win – they influenced the election. And that is my point in this book: these developers are controlling elections and in turn, receive "sweetheart deals" from various political entities that pads their wallets and enables them to control and dictate the configuration of the city (with the help of city planners, that is).

Black people are not above benefitting from racism. Because of its segregation Cincinnati tried to put a band-aid on it with a loan to a black woman who wanted to open a soul food restaurant. As Christian & Lake reported it:

> One of the largest, and most controversial, of the city's unpaid commercial loans was made was to Liz Rogers, owner of the failed Mahogany's restaurant at The Banks. In 2012 the city lent Rogers $300,000 and gave her a $684,000 grant **to help bring a minority-owned business to The Banks**. When the soul food restaurant struggled, **former City Manager Harry Black made a deal in 2015 to forgive almost all of the city money she received**, only asking Rogers to repay $100,000. To date, Rogers has repaid $3,200, and nothing since February 2016.

Remember that Harry Black is the brutha who was suing the mayor for "sweetheart deals." What gall.

But this is what happens in politics. The mayor gives his boys the jobs and in exchange his appointed City Manager gets a token chance to do the same thing for a black woman. The black woman, of course, goes under because a soul food restaurant on The Banks is like putting Black Panther headquarters on main street in Macon, Georgia. The Banks is lily-white and white folks want to keep it that way. And let me add the importance of the waterfront to the creation of this awesome business and residential area. History documents the following:

> The Banks development is a central element of downtown Cincinnati's riverfront revitalization, and has fulfilled the goal of becoming a catalytic economic engine. Spurred by $157 million in public infrastructure improvements, **the private joint venture team has invested more than $162 million in phase one, and $69 million in phase two, . Bringing new money to Cincinnati through the purchase of local goods and services and hiring local workers,** the operating impact of The Banks is a critical component to Cincinnati's success. Upon completion, the annual economic impact from phase one and two of The Banks is projected to be over $1.2 billion.(The Banks Cincinnati, 2018 – emphasis added)

The Soul Food Restaurant mentioned earlier used the argument that more minority businesses were need in this riverfront mecca. So when these writers (the previous excerpt is from the website) make claims about purchasing of local goods and services and "hiring local workers," the assumption is that the hiring will include people of color. In America it is never wise to make such an assumption.

Lexington Mayor's Race and the Developers

This book seeks to point to the pervasiveness of the mayor-developer relationships around America, which is why Lexington, Kentucky is one of the cities chosen. Lexington is a city with a population of 318,449. Lexington has an elected mayor-city council form of government.

We go to another recent election to get a picture of the role of developers in impacting on that election. A May 9, 2018 article by Tom Eblen headlined, "Mayor's Race Will Shape Lexington's Growth: Who is the Big Money Backing?" The article begins:

> When deciding which political candidate to vote for, **it is always smart to follow the money.** In the Lexington mayor's race, campaign contributions offer an interesting window into where contributors think the candidates stand **on the perennial hot-button issue of suburban expansion vs. farmland preservation**. (Eblen, 2018 – emphasis added)

Lexington is 13.5% African-American, so the suburban issue is important because any time a black population surpasses 5-6%, white folks begin to worry and then scurry. But development and "redevelopment" remain a priority for any administration:

> Depending who the next mayor is, Lexington could be in for big changes **after years of holding the line on expanding the Urban Services Boundary** and focusing on infill and redevelopment to protect the area's unique rural landscape. (Eblen, 2018 – emphasis added)

They "held the line" which means that the incoming mayor knows that he or she can "cut loose" when it comes to spending on infrastructure and redevelopment. The "unique rural landscape" is going to end up being nothing more than a tourist attraction that will surround an urban money making central business district.

The riverwalk is not much, but it is still promoted as a tourist attraction. As the website describes it,

> Did you know there is a creek beneath the city? **Lexington was founded on the banks of the Town Branch Fork of the Elkhorn River, which provided a source of freshwater for colonial settlers.** As the city grew, Lexington's relationship with Town Branch changed, **and the creek was buried below ground in two culverts.** Click the episodes along the culvert lines (shown in white) to listen to episodes **as you tread over the city's underground storm water system to investigate the history,**

> **ecology, geology and infrastructure that impact the city's hidden waterway.** (Town Brasnch Waterwalk, 2018)

No matter how small, the planners find a way to exploit the water in a given area. Back to the election:

> Seven candidates are running in the non-partisan May 22 primary. Four have a realistic chance of making it to the two-person general election Nov. 6. **The winner will succeed two-term Mayor Jim Gray, who is running for Congress.** Reports filed April 22 with the Kentucky Registry of Election Finance show distinct **contribution patterns with at least two candidates on development issues.** (Eblen, 2018 – emphasis added)

First, about Gray's bid for Congress. He lost in his bid for the Kentucky House. As reported on the website Vox.com,

> Insurgent candidate Amy McGrath, a retired Marine fighter pilot, pulled off an upset victory in a Democratic primary House race in Kentucky on Tuesday night, defeating the party establishment candidate.(Nilsen, 2018)

So Gray served two terms as Mayor, had his fun and then, probably because of term limits, decided he would move up a notch. But to no avail:

> McGrath emerged from a three-person race in Kentucky's Sixth District, beating her main challenger, Lexington Mayor Jim Gray. The race was called around 8 pm, with McGrath winning with 46 percent of the vote to Gray's 42.3 percent. **Gray, a millionaire who ran for US Senate against Rand Paul in 2016,** had the backing of the Democratic Congressional Campaign Committee. (Nilsen, 2018)

Obviously a professional politician, it is clear that Gray wasn't running just to get paid. Already a millionaire, one has to wonder how much he made off of "deals" with developers. And in Lexington, the developers surely make a difference:

> Kevin Stinnett, who has served 14 years on the Urban County Council, has raised $210,009. **He is the overwhelming choice of developers, real estate executives, property managers, bankers, real estate attorneys, architects and construction contractors**. (Eblen, 2018 – emphasis added)

That support did not do him any good. According to a news article, "Stinnett said negative editorials by the Herald-Leader helped contribute to his poor showing. "We had a lot of negative obstacles to overcome," Stinnett said. "We had a newspaper that was negative and singled me out and tried to attack me. We had an opponent who tried a smear campaign behind the scenes.. I didn't stoop to their levels. " Stinnett did not name the opponent who allegedly tried to smear him. (Musgrave & Ward, 2018)

Perhaps Stinnett pissed off some people when it became obvious that his expansion plan was a gift for developers. As one article explained the campaign before the election,

> One reason may be the unsuccessful amendment Stinnett proposed last November when the council narrowly voted to keep the current Urban Services Boundary intact. Stinnett said his amendment would give the city more "flexibility" on future expansion, but others saw it differently. "This is not flexibility," **Vice Mayor Steve Kay said at the time. "This is doing away with the boundary."** (Eblen, 2018 – emphasis added)

With the developers, real estate attorneys and others behind him, how could Stinnett lose? According to the news article prior to the election,

> Developers donating to Stinnett included Dennis Anderson, Woodford Webb, Jimmy Nash, Phil Greer, Patrick Madden, Andy Haymaker, Ralph Ruschell and Ron Turner. Some have posted big campaign signs for him on their commercial properties. Stinnett also got contributions from political action committees for homebuilders, Kentucky American Water Co. and the law firm Stoll Keenon Ogden. Retired water company president Roy Mundy and water contractor Warren Rogers also donated. (Eblen, 2018)

Stinnett lost because somebody held a grudge. It is clear that the developer community had his back. But in politics money is what counts but reputation also has a lot to do with it. If you piss off the wrong politicos or corporate types, those interlocking directorates can prove to be your undoing.

Perhaps Stinnett made too many "expansion" oriented promises too soon. For instance,

> Linda Gorton, who retired in December 2014 after 16 years on the council, including four years as vice mayor, raised $128,280. **She is the overwhelming choice of people who oppose expansion of the Urban Services Boundary, especially farm owners**. Gorton has been a longtime advocate for Fayette County's **$2.3 billion agriculture sector,**

> rural land preservation and urban infill and redevelopment. (Eblen, 2018
> – emphasis added)

The farm lobby, of course! That is one sector of the economy that has money but more importantly land. And everyone knows that land is power. So the developers were important but those hicks down at the farm were not going to back anybody who was about expansion of the Urban Services boundary which just might upset Corey the Cow, Greg the Goat and Patsy the Pig. Those farmers look out for their own!

As the article further explains it,

> **Well-known farm owners donating to Gorton** included Frank Penn, Josephine Abercrombie, Helen Alexander, Brutus Clay, Don Robinson and former Gov. Brereton Jones. Gorton's strongest support, totaling $12,000, came from Mt. Brilliant Farm owner Greg Goodman and his family. **There were only a few Gorton donors in real estate or development,** including Tim Haymaker and Robert Langley, both of whom gave equally to Gorton and Stinnett. (Eblen, 2018 – emphasis added)

It appears to me that the developers had their doubts and therefore split their donations, figuring that they would win in either case. But it was not to be. The farmers weren't playing around and a giant share of Lexington's reputation is rural-oriented. It should also be noted that,

> The council last year **approved a 5-year comprehensive land-use plan** that for the first time requires completion of a study by July 1, 2020 to determine triggers for **opening more rural land for development**. Who is appointed to that study committee — and whose interests they represent — could make a big difference in the study's outcome and future development decisions. (Eblen, 2018)

And that brings us back to the farm lobby. That comprehensive plan was calling for incursions onto farmland and that is what Stinnett was behind, or so it seemed. And that is why he lost.

<u>Palo Alto, (CA.) Mayor's Re-Election Bid and the Developers</u>

The election here is over, but the money kept pouring in. And that money was linked to developers. Remember this is Palo Alto, California, a small city we used to call "Nairobi" back in the black power days. But more importantly it is home to Stanford University. The election is a case study in the power of and relationship to developers when it comes to the mayor's office.

The story of the 2017 mayoral election begins with the following January article:

> Ten days after Liz Kniss cruised to an Election Day victory, picking up more votes than any other candidate, **contributions continued to flow into her campaign chest.** But unlike the checks that Kniss had received in the months leading up to Nov. 8, **most of the new contributions came from developers, builders and property managers, some of whom have been doing business in Palo Alto for decades**. (Sheyner, 2017 – emphasis added)

After-the-election donations continuing to pour in from developers, builders and property managers. One wonders why that would be the case – perhaps to curry favor with the city's new decision maker? Perhaps get some advantages in bidding for jobs and projects that will inevitably arise? What did they call it in the De Blasio case – "old machine politics"? This is the west coast and as you can see the process and procedures are still alive and well and focused on land development.

And,

> **A $500 contribution from developer and land-use consultant Jim Baer -- who has developed dozens of "planned community" projects** throughout Palo Alto -- was reported as having been received on Nov. 18. The same date is attached to a reported $2,500 contribution **from the California Association of Realtors** and a $1,000 contribution from Joseph Martignetti, board member at the **nonprofit Palo Alto Housing, which develops low-income housing**. (Sheyner, 2017 – emphasis added)

To begin with, generally speaking a "planned community is a housing development where the homes, roads, stores and other features are carefully designed and orchestrated to make living there as convenient and enjoyable as can be. The cost to live there is high which is the new way to make sure that only few minorities will be able to afford to live there. More simply and to the point, urban planning dictionaries define a planned community a residential district that is planned for a special "class" of people. In my view the term "class" can be replaced with the word "race" quite easily and appropriately.

Donations from the California Association of Realtors as well. Founded in 1905, this group is not just about land but also has a political action committee that spends money:

> The C.A.R. administers several political action committees to support candidates who agree with association goals or to engage ballot initiatives. CREPAC (California Real Estate Political Action Committee) is a bipartisan PAC that supports state candidates who support association policies. The LCRC (Local Candidate Recommendation Committee) has a fund within the CREPAC budget to support local candidates (California Association of Realtors website, 2018)

So this is how the game is played – even AFTER an election it's alright to offer a little "candy" to the person who won so that they will remember your name once the jobs come around the bend.

But that was not all:

> There was also a $999 contribution from Charles "Chop" Keenan, whose **downtown developments** include Whole Foods, Aquarius Theatre and the Varsity Theatre building that now houses Hana Haus. The check, **along with three other $999 checks from employees Keenan's company**, were all reported as having been received on Nov. 20. (Sheyner, 2017 – emphasis added)

And the money just kept on coming:

> **Thoits Brothers, a development firm,** contributed $1,875 to the Kniss campaign, and **Hatco Associates LLC -- an entity affiliated with Thoits -- gave another $1,250** (both were reported as received on Nov. 20). Other checks that, according to the Jan. 11 campaign filing, were received on Nov. 20 include **$999 from Premier Property** and **a pair of $250 contributions from two employees of Jones Lang LaSalle (a commercial real estate company).** Palo Alto Improvement Company gave $1,875, with the amount also reported on Nov. 20. (Sheyner, 2017 – emphasis added)

There was money to be made and these developers knew whose palms to grease in order to get what they believed was the "inside track." Remember: all this came AFTER Kniss had already won the election. More specifically,

> **Altogether, the 27 checks received between Nov. 18 and Nov. 26 total $19,340, with about $16,000 of the total coming from developers, builders and real estate professionals.** While the total is dwarfed by contributions that Kniss' opponents in last year's competitive council race received, these contributions stand out because -- unlike others **-- they weren't reported until well after residents cast their votes on Election Day.** (Sheyner, 2017 – emphasis added)

When the welfare system was in full throttle, all you heard these white people talking about was black women trying "to get something for nothing" or "taking advantage of the system." What do you think these developers are doing? First they use money to get the attention of the mayor. Then they wine and dine him or her and "beg" for a chance to receive priority treatment. Then they sit and wait for their bid on a particular project (welfare) to be granted so that they can feed their families and pay the mortgage on their gated community home. This is the real America, the one that the media doesn't want you to see.

Builders were evidently a part of the campaign concerns of those in the audience as well. According to Sheyner, (2017),

> **The contributions are also notable in another way.** Several candidates in the race -- most notably Greg Tanaka and Adrian Fine -- were assailed during the campaign **by their ideological opponents for receiving "too much" cash from builders.** Kniss, by contrast, was largely immune from these criticisms. Though she enjoyed an early fundraising lead in late September and early October, **developers made up only a tiny fraction of her supporters.** Instead, her list of contributors included former mayors, council members, business executives, neighborhood leaders and even some land-use watchdogs (Bob Moss among them). (emphasis added)

Developers may have only made up "a tiny fraction of her supporters," but the folks that supported her may have had connections. For instance, the excerpt says that her list of contributors included "Former mayors, council members, business executives, neighborhood leaders and even some land-use watchdogs." But these types are or may be directly or indirectly tied to developers. Even the "land use watch dogs" know who the developers are and if a developer sees that connection, they might contribute to her just to keep her off THEIR back. These interlocking partnerships can exist because these people are white and they live in the same areas of the city, attend the same social functions and their kids go to the same schools. These are facts that cannot and should not be ignored.

Continuing:

> State law requires candidates to report within 24 hours every contribution of $1,000 or more that comes from a single source. However, that requirement only applies to the period between Aug. 10 and Election Day. **Large contributions that the candidate received after Nov. 8 are not subject to the 24-hour rule.** They do, however, need to be listed on the campaign committee's semi-annual filing, which covers the period between Oct. 23 and Dec. 31. (Sheyner, 2017 - emphasis)

In other words those contributions were "gifts." The money represented free money to Kniss from those donors which went straight into her bank account. That is the kind of money that won't be forgotten and the donors knew it. These donors want her to remember them when she sees the name of their company on her "return this call" sheet once she takes office. That is why all these donations came on or near the same time because all the donors knew what time it was and what to do. Whoever won was going to get that money even if it wasn't Kniss. And yet, no harm, no foul – simply the "American way."

Therefore,

> When asked about the late reporting of the developers' contributions, Kniss said **her intent during most of the campaign was to avoid accepting money from builders.** But with candidates Arthur Keller and Lydia Kou -- who favor less aggressive city-growth policies -- receiving more than $100,000 from five local families and **her own campaign faced with a $20,000 deficit after Election Day**, Kniss changed her stance. "I think it was clear, since we ended up with two sides in the elections, **that they (the developers) were interested in supporting us,"** Kniss told the Weekly. **"And I was willing to be supported when I was $20,000 in the hole at that point."** (Sheyner, 2017 – emphasis added)

She was in on it all along and she came out looking like the hypocrite that she had always been in theory, but eventually revealed the fact in actual practice. She is no different than the others and now she knows where the real power lies. She will be in the hip pocket of those developers and they will get what they want after all. For instance, check out the following claim by one of the developers:

> **Yet several developers told the Weekly that they made their contributions well before the election.** Baer said he issued his check to Kniss on Oct. 26, nearly two weeks before Nov. 4. **Keenan also recalled that Kniss had asked him for money in the late days of the campaign and that he made the contribution shortly before Election Day. "She came to me late, saying, 'I want some dough. Can you help me?'"** Keenan said. "I said 'fine.' I couldn't respond right away because I was in the middle of a closing but I ultimately did. "I do remember that she didn't think she needed to raise the dough, **but then she realized that she did."** (Sheyner, 2017 – emphasis added)

Kniss was quite literally begging. Perhaps Keenan should not have shared that fact with the newspaper because when Kniss reads it she might be pissed about being portrayed as a desperate leech. But then again, she won the election so maybe she won't give a damn. The point here is that these politicians, these mayors of these cities will do what needs to be done to win, and developers and others know this quite well. And in turn, they will do whatever it takes to get a "desperado" into office so that they (the developers) can make deals and more importantly, make money.

Moving on:

> **There is nothing particularly surprising about the fact that developers supported Kniss in her re-election bid**. Since she re-joined the council in 2012, Kniss has had a mixed and moderate record on issues relating to growth. **She was part of the five-member majority to support new developments at 441 Page Mill Road and the former Olive Garden site on El Camino Real, both of which were approved by 5-4 votes**. But she also voted against a proposed Mercedes dealership in the Baylands and was in favor of an annual cap on new office development. (Sheyner, 2017)

What does such a record mean to me? It shows me that the ones who paid under the table and behind closed doors, the ones who wined and dined her or who drove out to her house and put a check on the table, were the ones who got the deals they wanted. On the other hand if you didn't make an offer, then she voted the other way. There is nothing mysterious about any of this, not even the cap that she voted to place on a new office development. An office development (too bland) or a Mercedes dealership (too elitist) – not sexy enough, not appealing enough to constituents. So it was no big deal to her. In addition, no offer was probably made.

Here is how she "explained" her strategy:

> In explaining her reluctance to solicit developer' contributions earlier in the campaign, **Kniss cited the negative perception that many in the community have of builders**. "One of the reasons I **really hesitated** on these contributions is because **developers really do feel that they are kind of second-class in many ways**," Kniss said. **"They are reviled, and it's a shame. I'm very aware that in this community, people are questioning developers' (contributions) like they're some sort of bad people."** (Sheyner, 2017 – emphasis added)

Kniss is trying to play both ends against the middle. On the one hand she talks about the "negative perception" that people in the community have of builders, and that negative perception, I might add, is deserved and earned. The masses know that developers are greedy assholes who over-charge poor people and make big money that is paid for by taxpayers on large projects. But then what does she turn around and do: accept their money once she wins.

But it's deeper than that. She adds that the developer is the one getting a raw deal and "it's a shame." She wants to stand up for them (or at least sound as if she is) so in case she needs their money in the future, she will not have burned any bridges. But she knows what these developers are about – that's why they become developers. Next to city planners, contractors and real estate speculators, the developer is about as low as you can get.

Moving on:

> She also noted that although at least some of the checks were sent in late October, they weren't reported until after the election because her campaign treasurer, Tom Collins, was undergoing rehabilitation after a surgery and was away from home for several weeks in early November. **Once he returned, he deposited the checks and reported them accordingly, she said**. (Sheyner, 2017 – emphasis added)

She's lying. She knows why those monies came in late and there were too many of them at the same time for it to be a coincidence or a fluke. She is as crooked as any of the other mayor's in America and there is no doubt that she is in the hip pocket of the developers. And there is a need for housing and a proposal signed for development of it – but it sounds like they only want a certain "class" of housing. According to one source from the Palo Alto News under the headline, "New Housing Laws Pose Planning Challenges For City, we find out the following:

> **The housing crunch may be an official Palo Alto priority, but City Hall wasn't cheering last week when Gov. Jerry Brown signed 15 bills that aim to encourage residential development.** State Senate Bill 35, which was sponsored by Scott Weiner, D-San Francisco, is among the most significant components in a package of housing bills that the Legislature approved in late September and that Brown subsequently signed into law on Sept. 29. **The bill creates a "streamlined" approval process for housing developers whose projects meet "objective" planning standards and include below-market-rate housing**. It is also the only housing bill that Palo Alto formally opposed. (Sheyner, 2017)

What is "below market-rate housing"? It's also known as "affordable housing" and it's for poor people. And Palo Alto is a racist city, no doubt about it. It is a city where the demographics show that it is lily white and it wants to remain that way: 75% white (58,595 residents), 17% Asian and there only 2% Black. Low income housing might bring in more "negroes" and these peckerwoods boast about being the home of Stanford University and that means white coeds prancing up and down the street. California may be considered liberal but outsiders, but I lived and grew up there: it is as racist as they come, only the leadership is what you might call "closet racists."

So Palo Alto opposes a bill that would bring in affordable housing, and yet still wants to spoon feed developers. You can run for office and talk about development without sounding racist, even when you are. For instance:

> **She also pointed to her record as proof that she hasn't been influenced by developer contributions and that she isn't "in the pockets" of developers.** Her contributors, she said, "wanted to support people who are interested in **Palo Alto continuing to thrive and they want to continue to do business here."** (Sheyner, 2017 – emphasis added)

When these white people said "go west, young man go west", and when the Gold Rush lured even more of them, who do you think took that advice and that imaginary road to riches? White people – racist white people. And these are their grandchildren and great grandchildren who are making these rulings and making statements about wanting a place to "thrive and continue to do business." These are the reasons they use to keep black people out of "their" communities and "their" districts and "their neighborhoods." Affordable housing, by way of apartments, raises the population density and attracts poor people, people who don't have the kind of money Palo Alto is looking for.

Lying ahead for Palo Alto is a "university avenue project" and a "downtown project," neither of which bodes well for increasing the numbers of black folks coming to town. Palo Alto does have a few powerful Asian members of the Common Council and they are saying the right things, but then again, most of them have been Americanized and just as there are black Oreos (black on the outside, white on the inside), and Latino "tio tacos", and First Nation apples (red on the outside, white on the inside) there are also Asian bamboo – yellow on the outside and hollow on the inside.

Remember that Stanford is no bastion of blackness, either. According to the university's own Access and Diversity office, the racial makeup of this internationally-known university is still lily white. Among staff that are non faculty, 45% re white and 3.8% are black, 22.95 are Asian and 11.4% are Hispanic. Among faculty only 2% are black. For graduate level students 2% are Black, 38% are white, 33% are International, 14% are Asian and 7% are Hispanic. For undergraduate students, 6% are black, 365 are white, 9% are international and 21% are Asian. There are more international students at Stanford than American-born blacks. Does Palo Alto sound like an inviting atmosphere to you?

<u>Fort Myers, (FL.) Mayor's Campaign Chest and theDevelopers</u>

The headline of the main article I am analyzing may well say it all about the mayor-developer relationship in that city of 48,208. The article from the July 20, 2017 edition of the *Fort Myers News-Press* by Cody Dulaney is titled, "One Quarter of Fort Myers Mayor's Campaign War Chest Traces to 3 Developers."

The article starts off like so:

> Mayor Randy Henderson has wasted no time raising cash for his re-election campaign, **bringing in nearly $62,000 with more than a month to go before the primary.** And about a quarter of that money **came from three developers**. Campaign contributions from an individual or business cannot exceed $1,000 in most local elections. But reports show **Henderson received 15 donations of $1,000 each from various shell companies and subsidiaries that are tied to those three people.** (Dulaney, 2017 – emphasis added)

Shell companies are also known as "shell corporations." Their function is usually to "hide" something. It has no real active business operation or any real assets; it's just there and is usually used for illegitimate purposes, to disguise ownership from the police or the public. They are legal but generate suspicion when used for election donation purposes. With a month ago this candidate for mayor gets all this money from all these "companies."

Dulaney (2017) writes that, "While that may not violate the law, experts say it violates the spirit of the law and it happens all the time. "It's nothing new whatsoever, and it's up to the voters themselves to become informed about who gives to a campaign and whether that matters or not," said Susan MacManus, a University of South Florida political science professor." And we all know the voters are as dumb as a bag of hammers. They don't care – many of them need help understanding how to pull a lever or push a button in a poll booth.

The political science professor continues by explaining, "People donate to a campaign for a variety of reasons, she said, but the movers and shakers within a community are often donating to establish a line of communication or ensure a seat at the table. (Dulaney, 2017) By a "seat at the table" she means input into development decisions that will be made. They want a piece of the pie and that will enable them to make money. This is how it is done, known as quid pro quo.

For instance,

> In June, **two developers doing business with the city split the cost of a $1,900 event to raise money for Henderson's re-election**, according to Henderson and campaign treasurer's reports. They are Randy Thibaut, **a real estate expert,** and Carl Barraco, who is behind **an 800-acre**

> **development on the corner of State Road 82 and Ortiz Avenue that
> will contain housing, retail and office space.** Companies controlled by
> the two men **also donated $500 apiece.** (Dulaney, 2017 – emphasis
> added)

These developers were already doing business with the city, so their
donation to Henderson should have been viewed as a conflict of interest. One of
the men has a major development going on that will generate a revenue stream
with rent, housing sales and rental of office space. So in other words they donated
to Henderson so that he could look the other way if need be or expedite some of
the many licenses that would be needed for such a gargantuan undertaking. This is
the real American way. So whether it's a mega-city like New York or Los Angeles,
or a hick town trying to be urbane like Omaha or Fort Myers, Florida, the white
man is always at work trying to circumvent the rules. This is at the base of the real
developer-mayor relationship.

Continuing:

> During that fundraiser, **seven companies that are controlled by Abel
> Ramirez each donated $1,000, reports show**. Ramirez is behind the
> **multi-million dollar Allure project, luxury high rises planned for the
> downtown riverfront.** His company is also responsible for bringing the
> **iron sculptures to downtown.** (Dulaney, 2017 – emphasis added)

This iron sculpture thing is what you can see in downtown Detroit and in
front of City Hall in Chicago. And many of them are worthless pieces of "art." But
as for that "fundraiser" (as they call it) where the seven companies donated a grand
each, that was a party. That was a "by invitations only" party that served enough
alcohol to drown a bear. And they were all there, no black folks around, partying in
their lily-white environment, cracking "nigga" jokes and writing out checks, glass
of Scotch in one hand, pen in the other hand signing for more Scotch.

But that wasn't all the money changing hands:

> In addition, **five donations of $1,000 each are all linked to Jadon Hull
> and companies controlled by the Hull family.** They are behind AIM
> Engineering, **a company with massive road projects all over the state,
> including the $430 million Interstate 75 widening between Fort
> Myers and Naples, and another road project near Miami
> International Airport**, in which the company beat out global
> engineering firms, according to the Business Observer. AIM
> Engineering, though, is not listed as a contributor. (Dulaney, 2017)

It's all in the family. And then these Black contractors go around whining
why they can't get bids in, are not informed of the letting of the bids or why they

never outbid the white firms. It's because of the "fundraising party" that I shared earlier, and it's because of the interlocking directorates that these white folks all share. They talk on the phone, play golf together and have little leisure activities that they all participate in. Then that take all that to the job and continue the phone conversations where they talk about who gets how big of a slice of the pie.

Residential segregation continues but has slowly declined. Racial segregation continues but is now much more shrouded in bullshit all white relationships like the ones I've alluded to. The white country club still exists, only with a small black token presence of people like Tiger Woods who are mixed race and could care less about the black community. And so the configuration of the roadways, buildings and housing developments remain in the hands of the white man unless he needs a minority "front" because of some unanticipated "inspection" that comes along that they weren't forewarned about.

The money just kept on coming. Again, Dulaney writes that, "In May, three donations of $1,000 each are linked to Charlie Huether, a Fort Myers businessman involved in a deal with the city several years ago that drew the attention of the FBI. None of the contributors above responded to multiple requests for comment. (Dulaney, 2017) What I am describing and have already made clear is echoed in the following passage:

> **These kinds of contributions are an age-old tactic to circumvent laws limiting the amount of money a person or business can donate to a political campaign,** MacManus said, and **people are becoming frustrated with the impact money has on politics.** But Henderson said there's nothing wrong with it. **Campaign contributions are a form of speech,** he said, and "you just have to be vigilant in making sure you do things appropriately, and I think that's the key." (Dulaney, 2017 – emphasis added)

And black people (the ones who don't study) wonder why there is a dearth of black representation on these various councils and why the black neighborhoods remain static while the rest of the community prospers. The previous passage said it all with the phrase, "age-old tactic." White people are doing it to each other even when black people are not a part of the equation. That is the purpose of white supremacy – to build and maintain "whiteness" by any means necessary.

It's about race-first – and THEN about the money, despite the claims in the following paragraph:

> **Money in politics is a problem, Henderson agreed, but not at the local level.** There are about 27,000 registered voters in the city and "it's not cheap to reach them," he said. "This has been characteristic of just about every campaign I've ever run … people support me in the best

way that they can," **said Henderson, who collected about $68,000 and $76,000 in his two previous campaigns**. (Dulaney, 2017 – emphasis added)

Henderson claimed that money in local politics is not a problem. But everyone even remotely involved in civics or government knows that "all politics is local." It's local racists who amass votes and determine the winner of the electoral college. It's the local hicks who vote in governors, congresspersons and senators. The local butthead who has money has an impact and imprint on the national picture. This has been proven time and time again as hicks like Gerald Ford, Ben Nelson, Ben Sasse, Bob Kerrey and other farmer types end up in Washington, DC from Nebraska. And when they get there, you hardly ever hear from them again. They have been paid for – in full.

Donations are the name of the game, even in Fort Myers, Florida – or so it seems:

> But Henderson isn't alone. Councilwoman Teresa Watkins-Brown, who is seeking her third term, has also accepted similar donations. **Four companies that are controlled by Brian Lucas, another developer doing business with the city, each donated $1,000 to Watkins-Brown's re-election campaign.** She has raised $8,925. Watkins-Brown said she knows of Lucas but doesn't know him personally, and wasn't aware those four companies linked back to him. **She disputed the notion that campaign contributions are an investment for developers "Why would you think (Lucas) wants to receive something in return?" Watkins-Brown said**. (Dulaney, 2017 – emphasis added)

Another white woman batting her eyes and claiming ignorance of what everybody else can see (remember the statement by Serena Oberstein from Los Angeles). Who in America gives something and expects nothing in return? And if she accepted it, why did she do so? Is she a leech? Didn't her mother teach her about accepting money from "strange men"? (She claims she didn't know them, remember?)

But we know the truth and by "we" I'm talking about scholars and thinkers such as myself. As Dulaney (2017) points out,

> **But that's exactly what it is — an investment, said Peter Bergerson, a political science professor at Florida Gulf Coast University**. He has taught public policy for nearly 50 years. **Local and state governments have been debating campaign finance laws for decades, but they likely won't change anytime soon,** Bergerson said. "Campaign finance laws are written by incumbents, for incumbents and to the advantage of

incumbents," he said. "So there's always going to be loopholes."
(emphasis added)

The key terminology in the preceding excerpt is, "debating campaign finance laws for decades." How could that be unless someone was pulling some major strings? Could it be that campaign finance laws are as American as apple pie and that the "debates" are nothing but a façade to hide the real importance of money in the political process?

Palm Springs, (CA.) Mayor and 2 Developers Charged

Palm Springs, a destination city for a lot of people across America. A city with a population of 42,807. And yet the power and impact of local developers rings just as loudly in this small California city as it did in New York.

In February of 2017 it was reported that both the former mayor and two developers were charged with corruption that involved $375,000 in bribes. Following is the article and my analysis of the situation.

According to Winton (2017),

> As Palm Springs' chief booster for nearly a decade, **former Mayor Steve Pougnet came to define the city's hunger for development and renewed prosperity.** In recent years, the town, once a favorite desert watering hole that attracted visitors from around the globe, has boomed, **with cranes dotting the skyline and the hum of construction competing with desert winds.** (Winton, 2017 – emphasis added)

The key is in the fact that the former mayor "came to define the city's hunger for development and renewed prosperity." The fact of the matter is that hunger had probably already been defined, and Pougnet, who served for eight years - just came along and expertly exploited it. First, he met with some development cronies. Then they figured out how the money would be divided and how best to keep what they were doing behind closed doors even as Pougnet spread the word that he was changing the skyline of the city. And then, the fix was in.

In other words,

> **But some of that expansion may be tainted, said prosecutors**, who on Thursday **accused Pougnet of accepting $375,000 in bribes from two developers whose projects he promoted.** Pougnet, 53, and developers Richard Meaney, 51, and John Wessman, 78, **were charged with a**

combined 30 felony counts of corruption, including paying and accepting bribes, conflict of interest, perjury and conspiracy to commit bribery. Pougnet served as mayor for eight years before stepping down in 2015. . (Winton, 2017 – emphasis added)

What a killing this trio made! And they got away with it in a city as small as Palm Springs, where gossip usually travels fast. But that gossip can be quelled and suppressed if the "planning" is taking place behind closed doors "amongst friends." As a result, "Pougnet faces up to 19 years in state prison, while the two developers face up to 12 years each behind bars. The trio is expected to surrender to authorities within days. "We simply cannot tolerate corruption in government at any level," Dist. Atty. Mike Hestrin said at a news conference. "With all bribery, it was about buying influence." . (Winton, 2017)

The district attorney is saying what he was supposed to say. He didn't say "accept" or "allow" corruption in government – he said "tolerate." And there's a big difference. Tolerate means that they can look the other way if they can somehow benefit. Tolerate means "to put up with." But to not put up with something is not the same as seeking to bring an end to it. You can "not put up" with your white daughter dating a black boy, but saying that and not putting an end to it means that she's going to keep doing it because the behavior was more beneficial than the shallow "threat" she received as a punishment. It works the same way in the developer-mayor relationship.

Furthermore, "Wessman, the city's biggest developer, along with Meaney paid bribes to gain influence in City Hall and beyond, Hestrin said. "This was a bribe and not just business," the prosecutor said. "It was pretty brazen, and it was pretty obvious." . (Winton, 2017). If it was so brazen and obvious, why didn't the district attorney uncover it before? Why didn't some members of the city administration blow the whistle on what Pougnet was doing?

How was it done?

Hestrin said money was funneled to the former mayor through a shell company from September 2012 to September 2014. The charges come 17 months after investigators from the FBI and the Riverside County district attorney's office seized documents from City Hall and the mayor's home as part of a public corruption investigation. . (Winton, 2017)

Here we go again with the "shell companies" that we discussed elsewhere. It took a 17-month investigation and in the meantime who knows how much money Pougnet blew on luxury items? The FBI went to his house and got some documents, so they knew he was the ringleader. After all, according to the article, "City incentives in recent years have spurred hundreds of millions of dollars in investments that are transforming the landscape of the desert city in the heart of the Coachella Valley. (Winton, 2017)

And it appears that the former mayor (perhaps in collusion with the current mayor?) had other projects taking place around the city known as "The Golf Capital of the World":

> The investigation has already **cast a shadow over a \$300-million retail, restaurant, office and hotel project designed to reshape downtown Palm Springs.** The city invested \$43 million in the venture, which involves replacing a decaying mall. **Wessman's company and the city are partners in the project. "Unfortunately for Palm Springs … there's going to be some difficulties in untangling this," Hestrin said.**
> . (Winton, 2017 – emphasis added)

Take note of the claim of re-shaping downtown Palm Springs. Again, that seems to be an obsession with mayors no matter what the venue. They want to change that skyline. And that obsession with bricks-and-mortar has proven to be the undoing of more than a few of the city leaders around the country, only a small number of them mentioned in this book.

In terms of the former Palm Springs mayor,

> **Pougnet is charged with nine counts of receiving bribes, eight counts of conflict of interest as a public official and three counts of perjury, plus an allegation of conspiracy to commit bribery.**The ex-mayor received nine payments and cast 11 votes on projects connected to the developers that required City Council approval, prosecutors said … **Pougnet, prosecutors said, did not reveal the payments and connections on his annual conflict-of-interest forms as required by law.** "This is a large amount of money that was **paid to the mayor for his influence on the City Council,"** Hestrin said. "The mayor is very influential, and these individuals had a lot to gain." . (Winton, 2017)

Influence over the City Council. And he exercised it. Now the question is what was their "cut"? They didn't vote his way for free. Did they have their own piece of the pie reserved for them or was their "reward" to come later? The Palm Springs raid scenario continues:

> The Sept. 1, 2015, raids came after a series of articles in the Desert Sun newspaper **showed that Pougnet, while mayor, worked as a consultant for Meaney during the same period he voted to sell city property to the developer and another investor**. After the Desert Sun in 2015 revealed that Pougnet received more than \$200,000 — now alleged to be \$375,000 — from firms run by Meaney, **Pougnet claimed**

he'd been hired to educate the developer on local development laws. .
(Winton, 2017 – emphasis added)

Double dipping and a definite conflict of interest. But what a well thought out scam. Had it not been for Desert Sun reporters doing their due diligence, Pougnet might have gotten away with it. Furthermore,

> In the wake of the public corruption probe, **Pougnet said his vote to approve the sale to Meaney of a 29,185-square-foot property called Casa Del Camino was a mistake**. Besides the property deal, Meaney also benefited from a **$250,000 city economic development grant** meant to help redevelop vacant properties — a vote from **which Pougnet abstained**, according to city records. . (Winton, 2017 – emphasis added)

More likely than not that grant came from Community Development Block Grant funds, and the mayor need not be present to vote. That decision is made by whoever is in charge of the Planning Department and more than likely there is a council subcommittee called the Planning Committee. It is quite logical that Pougnet "gave the word" to his supporters in both entities to vote positive when Meaney's proposal came forth. That's how it works.

As for his "after the fact" claim that approving the sale of the 29,000 square foot property to Meaney was "a mistake," what do you expect him to say? As a matter of fact, by saying that such a major transaction constituted a "mistake" is even WORSE than had it been done on purpose because the decision shows that Pougnet is an idiot who did not deserve to be in a mayoral position!

> In a statement, Michael Braun, senior vice president of Wessman Development said that as of Wednesday, Wessman had retired from his position as president of the company and was no longer involved in management or day-to-day operations. "**While John Wessman denies all of the allegations of the complaint, which he will vigorously defend, the paramount concern of John Wessman, Michael Braun, all of the Wessman entities and the entirety of the staff, is to ensure that all projects proceed in a timely manner to completion,**" Braun said. . (Winton, 2017 – emphasis added)

This is what these cowardly white boys do. When they get caught they step down and claim not to be involved in "day-to-day operations." That's what Trump did when he took office, but he still ran Trump Enterprises from behind closed doors. That's what these white boys do so that they can maintain their projects and insure that their buddies and pals (read: employees) continue to get paid.

Moving right along:

> Malcolm Segal, Pougnet's attorney, said he had yet to examine specifics
> of the charges. But he said his client properly disclosed his income and is
> "really saddened" by the allegations. "Steve Pougnet always did his best
> for the people of Palm Springs," Segal said. "He made every financial
> disclosure required of him and did so truthfully. **He worked very hard
> to bring downtown Palm Springs back during his years in office."** .
> (Winton, 2017 – emphasis added)

"Worked very hard to bring Palm Springs back." Back from what? The edge of doom? The precipice of a zombie apocalypse? What? Palm Springs has always been a destination city, so it wasn't doing too bad. The nickname – the Golfing Capital – is not a nickname given to some hole-in-the wall slum. So that "bringing Palm Springs back" is bullshit. Pougnet, like any mayor in America, is out there to expand on what already exists, to improve the skyline and to add to tourist attractions. Read about these other cities and developers in these other cities that I have included in this book and you'll see what I mean.

The attorney continues his befuddled babbling as follows:

> The attorney said it would be a mistake to believe that Pougnet alone
> could steer City Council decisions. **"He was just one vote of five on
> every decision by the City Council," Segal said**. Pougnet first joined
> **the council in 2003 and became mayor in 2007**. After the 2015 raids,
> he declared, "I am happy to cooperate with the inquiry going on at City
> Hall, just as I have always been fully cooperative and open in all of my
> many years as an elected official in Palm Springs." . (Winton, 2017 –
> emphasis added)

These are long-term relationships. He serves with the council and then runs for mayor with the support of at least some of them – perhaps all. With that in mind there was no issue of "steering" Council members. There are ways to work out payola without direct involvement. He could have paid them under the table or offered them some other incentive. Pougnot's attorney is an idiot.

Everybody knew as the article implies, a point that is somewhat reiterated in the closing passage:

> **The charges came as no surprise to some City Hall watchers who
> said developers wield too much influence** over how public dollars are
> spent in the desert town, which was once **a playground for Hollywood's
> biggest celebrities.** "I am thankful they have finally brought the
> charges," said Judy Deertrack, an attorney who works on development
> issues. "The city has been under a cloud of uncertainty for the last 17
> months." . (Winton, 2017)

Again, the claim that Pougnet was going to "bring Palm Springs back" is disproven. You've seen the old TV shows and even hear, from time to time, the promotion of Palm Springs. The developers wanted to make money changing the skyline and the mayor was working with them to do just that.

Moving from the west coast down to the south east, we find that collusion between the mayor and developers is a nationwide phenomenon. This point will be analyzed in the following case of Hallandale Beach, Florida and the issue of "political favors."

Hallandale Beach, (FL.): Longtime Mayor and 2 Developers Charged With Collusion

Collusion is as big a part of the mayor's office of American cities, large and small, as a bat is to the game of baseball. It's rampant to the point where it appears to be almost a necessity.

According to Bryan & McMahon (2018), 57-year-old Joy Cooper was accused of meeting with "wealthy land developers who were actually undercover FBI agents pretending to seek political favor for a project in Hallandale Beach. The facts of this story appeared in the January 26, 2018 issue of the local paper, the Fort Lauderdale Sun-Sentinel.

Beginning:

> **Longtime Hallandale Beach Mayor Joy Cooper** has been freed from jail after her arrest in a public corruption case linked to disbarred Hollywood attorney Alan Koslow. Cooper, 57, was charged with three felonies Thursday, **accused of meeting with wealthy land developers who were actually undercover FBI agents pretending to seek political favor for a project in Hallandale Beach**. (Bryan & McMahon, 2018 – emphasis added)

Once again, the wealthy land developer has colluded with a top official or a group of them in an effort to gain an advantage and make millions of dollars behind the backs of the everyday citizenry. Getting caught in the act is embarrassing and there will be no chance for ever holding a public office again, despite the easily assembled lies of attorneys and supporters.

Continuing:

> She is alleged to have solicited and **accepted $5,000 in political campaign contributions from them that were funneled to her through Koslow, court records show.** The agents met with Cooper and

Koslow over the course of several months in 2012 as part of a public corruption sting and the meetings were all recorded on audio or video, court records say. (Bryan & McMahon, 2018 k- emphasis added)

The amount is not much, but Hallandale Beach is not a large area. The population is only 38,951 and is 74% white and 18.5% Black. Such gall did these people have that they were cutting deals in the City Hall building. According to the article,

> **Cooper, who turned herself in to jail officials Thursday morning, was charged with money laundering, official misconduct and exceeding the limit on campaign finance contributions**. Each carries a maximum five-year prison sentence. She also has been charged with **soliciting contributions in a government building** first-degree misdemeanor with a maximum one-year sentence. "We look forward to our day in court and the mayor's vindication," said her attorney, Larry Davis. "We're extremely disappointed that the Broward County State Attorney's Office is relying upon Alan Koslow, a disgraced and disbarred convicted felon, as the centerpiece of its case of alleged campaign finance violations." (Bryan & McMahon, 2018 – emphasis added)

How can you be vindicated when you were caught in the act by undercover FBI agents? She's got the money to defend herself with, if posting bail is any indicator:

> **Cooper, wearing a black dress, walked out of the downtown Fort Lauderdale jail on Thursday evening after posting $12,000 bond** just before 7 p.m. She briefly stopped in front of the TV news cameras, and let Davis, who was standing next to her, speak on her behalf. "We have no further comment at this point. We'll see you guys in court," Davis told the media. "Thanks very much." Cooper didn't comment, but nodded as Davis spoke. **A few steps from the jail, Davis opened a car door for Cooper. She got into the car's back seat to be driven away.** (Bryan & McMahon, 2018 – emphasis added)

Koslow was one of the people that was with the mayor when they were busted. And he is the link to the developers:

> Koslow, 63, was considered one of the most effective and best-known attorneys and lobbyists in the state, **specializing in representing developers and the gaming industry.** He pleaded guilty in August 2016 to helping people prosecutors said he thought were "quasi-mafia" **criminals hide the source of $220,000 linked to illegal gambling and drug dealing**. (Bryan & McMahon, 2018 – emphasis added)

Either you're in organized crime or you're not – there is no "quasi-Mafia," that Koslow knows it. He simply didn't want to name the names of the 'upright citizens' who were stashing money behind closed doors. Drug dealing and illegal gambling – so he must have cut a deal and snitched on Cooper. Some background is provided:

> **The FBI's sting began in 2012 and was turned over to state prosecutors in May 2017**, said Constance Simmons, a spokeswoman for the Broward State Attorney's Office. **Undercover FBI agents, posing as land developers from California "seeking political favor" for development projects,** hired Koslow to represent them, court records show. "At this time, Alan Koslow was unaware that he was interacting with undercover Federal Bureau of Investigation agents," investigators wrote. (Bryan & McMahon, 2018 – emphasis added)

What difference does it make if he knew or didn't know that they were FBI. They came to him for help and wanted to "engage" decision makers for some other than legitimate deals. Koslow was willing to comply because his reputation probably proceeded him – he had experience with drug deals and gambling, so he no stranger to hiding money and identities.

But the FBI, despite taking their time making the final bust, was taking their time "setting up" the mayor and Koslow:

> Cooper, mayor since 2005, and Koslow **were secretly recorded during numerous meetings and conversations, court documents show**. Koslow had **told the undercover agents he had influence with the mayor and city commissioners** and that he "had the vote of the mayor," the records show. (Bryan & McMahon, 2018 – emphasis added)

So then it mattered not if he knew they were FBI or not. He was boasting about his "connections" and he knew that what he was saying was illegal at worst, unethical at best. And mayor Cooper was also fully aware of what time it was when she sat down with the undercover agents:

> During a meeting July 10, 2012 between Cooper, the undercover agents and Koslow at City Hall, **Cooper was recorded saying that she and two other commissioners were a "team of three"** and could **ensure a favorable result for their project**, according to the arrest affidavit. "Alan Koslow showed Mayor Cooper a number representing a proposed contribution and asked her if it was a good number. She replied 'No. Add a zero." Koslow confirmed **'Three zeros, is that fine?' and Mayor Cooper replied 'Yes,'" according to the arrest affidavit**. (Bryan & McMahon, 2018 – emphasis added)

"A team of three." "Ensure a favorable result." Remember what I've been writing about these "interlocking directorates" and how these white people interact with one another? This has been going on for centuries in this country even while all this talk about "good government" is bandied about on the news programs and in the newspapers. The media is fully aware when things aren't going right downtown, but they feed off of controversy and if they act as whistleblowers, they will be cut off from getting essential stories and leads from local government. That's how it has worked since the days of the penny press. And it's lily-white in most cases. When black people win mayoral elections, most of them mimic what their white predecessors did so if caught, they can point the finger.

The mayor-developer case in Hallandale Beach continues:

> Later that month, **Koslow told Cooper she would receive $10,000 in the form of two $5,000 contributions – one before the August 2012 primary and one after,** the records state. In August 2012, Koslow and the agents **went to Cooper's home.** After that meeting, **the agents went to Koslow's home and gave him a Dunkin' Donuts bag that contained $8,000 in cash,** investigators said in court records. Koslow had told the **agents he would have two Russian organizations write checks for them, investigators wrote.** (Bryan & McMahon, 2018 – emphasis added)

What? Russian organizations? But remember this: Russians are white just like the real "Americans" are. They are brothers despite their ideological differences. And this has been the case all along. But the point I want to make is just look at the "home visits" that these developers can make with those involved in the scam. This is again the "interlocking directorate" based on race, at work. This is why they don't get caught: it's personal and social, not just political.

And this is why segregation is so important. Living way out behind those gated community security shields, you can pick and choose who gets in or out, or who you live next to, or who can see who's "coming and going." Whites back whites and they don't have to worry about a "minority do-gooder" upsetting the apple cart.

Continuing:

> During a recorded **meeting at the Flashback Diner** on Aug. 20, 2012, one of the undercover agents told Cooper that "the pledged payment to her, via her campaign, **would be in the form of checks from a 'bunch of Russian names,'"** according to court documents. (Bryan & McMahon, 2018 – emphasis added)

The Flashback Diner. This was of concern to me so I did some research on the internet. First of all it's along the Federal Highway. It's also open 24 hours and get this: it serves beer and wine. So this is not some celery and garnish meeting. These people are probably meeting in the wee hours on some highway-type eatery and are getting blitzed while they're meeting. Add the Russian angle to this, and you have the makings of a real cloak and dagger spy story. After all, what is there to hide?

> In September, Koslow told one of the agents **he had personally handed 20 checks to Cooper at a Hallandale Beach Chamber of Commerce fashion show,** court records say. The checks, totaling $5,000, were broken down into smaller amounts that appeared to come from people with Russian last names, according to the documents. Cooper said "that's fantastic" when she got the checks, according to what Koslow told the undercover agents. (Bryan & McMahon, 2018 – emphasis added)

So she's meeting at a public event and getting "slipped" envelopes filled with checks. But checks leave a paper trail, Russian names or not. In fact that seems much worse than straight up cash payments. But these people have been doing this for so long they know which venues to meet at, which are the best times, and how to get the checks from one hand to another. And the public is apparently none the wiser.

The developers also masked their donations. For instance,

> Cooper's campaign reported nine contributions **from eight teachers and a retired person in the amount of $500 each, matching names on a list of donors Koslow had given the so-called developers**, the affidavit said. "You guys have been great," Cooper told the undercover agents during a meeting with Koslow at the **Flashback Diner on Oct. 3, 2012,** court documents state. **She told them one of the checks had bounced.** (Bryan & McMahon, 2018 – emphasis added)

The Flashback Diner seems to be a favorite haunt of these crooks. And the meetings were on-going and frequent, according to the records:

> According to federal court records, **Koslow met at least 75 times with four different FBI agents between September 2013 and May 2016,** though what he did remains secret because of continuing investigations. **Koslow gave a sworn statement to investigators Nov. 9, 2017 – after he was released from federal prison and a halfway house – acknowledging that he participated in all of the recorded events.** (Bryan & McMahon, 2018 – emphasis added)

Seventy five times in just under three years – that's about 25 times per year. And no one was none the wiser? This must be a very sleepy town because at very least the employees at the diner should have been getting suspicious. But remember: these are white people and they do what it takes to protect their own for the most part. That is why whistleblowers are so rare. The same race of people that in 2018 is calling the cops on a black person walking down the street, or a group of blacks having a picnic in a park, or a black employee getting out of her car at work, are the same ones who turn a blind eye to repetitive meetings of white people in a diner whispering and passing envelopes.

And though busted, look at the immediacy with which the governor acted. According to Bryan (2018) it was a 24- dismissal:

> Voters in Hallandale Beach will choose two commissioners and a new mayor in November, **nearly a year after Joy Cooper's political downfall. Cooper, mayor since 2005, was arrested Jan. 25 on felony charges after being snared in an FBI sting. She was removed from office the next day by Gov. Rick Scott**. (Bryan, 2018 – emphasis added).

The long-time mayor fell hard it appears. And the controversy that usually surrounds Hallandale Beach elections continues because,

> Her longtime nemesis, Keith London, was vice mayor at the time and inherited her seat. Cooper's arrest and the resignation of Anthony Sanders in August — more than a year before the end of his term — set off a series of musical chairs on the five-member commission. (Bryan, 2018)

A political upheaval, courtesy of whom? Developers and a mayor. Continuing:

> **London took on Cooper for the mayor's seat in 2012 and lost, but he returned to the commission two years later.** Now London's **hoping voters keep him in the mayor's seat when they head to the polls on Nov. 6.** Political newcomer **Joy Adams, who has sparred with London from the audience, is also running**. (Bryan, 2018 – emphasis added)

Out with the old and in with the new. But one thing that does not change is the vision, intention and motivations of developers. And there is plenty of political misfeasance to go around:

> **The 4-square-mile city is not divided into voting districts, so
> elections are citywide.** Hallandale Beach**, already known for
> its feisty politics,** found itself under an even more intense media glare
> in the past year. Sanders, a longtime commissioner, resigned his seat
> last year after **being accused by the Inspector General of using his
> elected position for financial gain**. Cooper's arrest only added to the
> intrigue. (Bryan, 2018 – emphasis added)

They all seem to be trying to get their piece of the rock. The formula seems
to be run for office, get elected and then try to find a developer to "adopt" you.
After that it's just a matter of locating a meeting place and getting paid by check.
As for Hallandale Beach, "The winner of the mayor's race will serve until
Cooper's term ends in 2020. If she is acquitted and returned to office before then,
the winner would be forced to step down. (Bryan, 2018)

Malcolm X taught that, "Of all our studies, history is best qualified to reward
our research." Little known Hallandale Beach has had more than its share of
political controversies as the following excerpt explains:

> **Cooper's arrest is the latest stain on a city that continually finds
> itself embroiled in controversy**. Former Commissioner Anthony
> Sanders **stepped down last year after being accused of misconduct by
> the Broward Inspector General**. In November, Cooper's political rivals
> — London and Commissioner Michele Lazarow — sent a letter to Gov.
> Scott asking him to remove her from office. Their letter came two days
> **after Cooper slurred her words at a commission meeting and
> appeared to be under the influence of "some behavior-altering
> substance," the letter said**. Cooper said she was not drunk or on meds
> but severely dehydrated after contracting diarrhea during a trip to
> Mexico. (Bryan & McMahon, 2018 – emphasis added)

Blame it on Mexico ("don't drink the water"). Maybe it was from one too
many trips to the Flashback Diner! The point to be made here is that these politicos
all seem to be on the take and for different reasons. For instance,

> **More than a year ago, London, Lazarow and Anabelle Taub — who
> was running for commission at the time and later won election —
> accused Cooper and other political rivals of spying on them**. Just two
> weeks before the city's November 2016 election, **London found a GPS
> tracker on his car**. Similar **tracking devices were found on cars
> owned by Lazarow and Taub**. At the time, **Cooper questioned
> whether London, Lazarow and Taub planted the trackers on their
> own cars as a political stunt**. (Bryan & McMahon, 2018 – emphasis
> added)

GPS tracking devices? Clandestine meetings at roadside diners? Accusations of a mayor being on some kind of behavior-altering drug? And this in a town of less than 40,000? The developer-mayor relationship is one that gets attention locally but apparently only after the money has changed hands and the construction has started. Where are the RICO (Racketeer-Influenced and Corrupt Organization) charges? Russians are involved even in this tiny city, so that is going on in the larger ones. Again, remember the words of Machiavelli: "Power corrupts, and absolute power corrupts absolutely."

Boca Raton (FL.) and Mayor-Developer Collusion

Next on our list is Boca Raton which is, like Palm Springs, another one of those tourist vacation spots. It is also a city that is only twenty-six (26) miles from Hallandale Beach, a town we just dealt with. The city has a population of 87,167.

In April of 2018 it was reported that the mayor of Boca Raton was arrested for accepting "improper funds" from, you guessed it – a developer. Let's dig in as the article informs us that,

> **Boca Raton Mayor Susan Haynie was arrested April 24 for allegedly failing to disclose income she received from a developer whose projects she favored in city council votes.** The charges by the Palm Beach County State Attorney's Office accuse **Haynie, who was first elected in 2014, of failing to disclose income from her private businesses and concealing payments to one business from developer James Batmasian.** During her time as mayor, **Haynie voted on several matters involving Batmasian's property.** (Bandell, 2018 – emphasis added)

Developers and their inducements. It is clear that these developers know how and where to "meet" with these mayors. This may be a pre-election arrangement but again, as I've stated throughout this book, the issues of race and class create a set of "interlocking directorates" that create a racial clique between all political aspirants, electorally speaking and those involved with the politics of land use and development.

Updated information reveals that Governor Scott did indeed remove Haynie from her position. More on that later. At any rate,

> According to multiple media reports, she dropped out of the running for a Palm Beach County Commission seat. **Gov. Rick Scott has the authority to suspend government officials who are charged with felonies.** He has yet to make an announcement regarding Haynie.

> **Haynie is charged with official misconduct, perjury in an official proceeding, misuse of public office, and corrupt misuse of public office, and failure to disclose a voting conflict, a misdemeanor.** (Bandell, 2018 – emphasis added)

Not only should she be removed from office, but she should perhaps be doing some serious jail time, especially with the amount of money involved.

> According to the probable cause affidavit from the State Attorney's Office, **Haynie and her husband, Neil Haynie, were the managing members of both Community Reliance LLC and Computer Golf Software of Nevada Inc.** Batmasian and his company **paid Community Reliance at least $12,000 a year to manage his condos in the Tivoli Park building.** Haynie did not disclose the payments from Batmasian through Community Reliance on her financial disclosures to the state as part of the requirements of holding public office, according to the state attorney. (Bandell, 2018 – emphasis added)

But there's more:

> The state investigator also found **Community Reliance received rent payments for a property in Key Largo that weren't disclosed**. In all, **$225,932 in payments were received by the company's Bank of America account from March 2014 through 2017**. In another account at Wells Fargo Bank, **Community Reliance received about $56,000 in payments from the Tivoli Park building from 2014 through 2017, and an additional $83,000 in payments from other Batmasian companies in 2016 and 2017**. (Bandell, 2018 – emphasis added)

These white folks, man and wife, were swimming in money, while 9.3% of the city's population is at or below the poverty level. It was like a blank check for Haynie. One article notes that, "The state attorney alleged that Haynie used the Computer Golf Software account to write checks to herself, and received $72,600 in income from it. The investigator determined that she had beneficial ownership of the accounts for both Community Reliance and Computer Golf Software." (Bandell, 2018)

`Another article provides additional information, as follows:

> "It is in the best interests of the residents of the City of Boca Raton, and the citizens of the State of Florida, that Susan Ince Haynie be immediately suspended from the public office, which she now holds, upon the grounds set forth in this executive order," Scott's order said. … About 30 minutes after Scott declared Haynie's suspension, the city of **Boca Raton announced that Deputy Mayor Scott Singer would serve**

> **as mayor until a special election on Aug. 28. This is in accordance with the city charter.** "We've been through some trying days; we will move forward," Singer said at brief press conference Friday evening. **"Business has continued as usual and there will be no interruption."** (Shatzman, 2018 – emphasis added)

The statement that "business has continued as usual and there will be no interruption" could mean a lot of things. But for those vulture-like developers who are sitting in wait, there can be no doubt what their next move will be: onward and upward! And the vultures aren't only in the developer's ranks, either. Check it out:

> Because Singer's move to the mayor's seat will create a vacancy on the council, the council, by majority vote, can appoint a qualified person to temporarily fill the opening until the election. **Singer had already filed to run for Haynie's seat.** (Shatzman, 2018)

Will Singer be a reflection of Haynie? Time will tell the tale. At any rate Haynie saw the writing on the wall before she was booted out:

> Haynie's arrest came as a shock to staff and other council members, who were **in the middle of a City Council meeting when she turned herself in to the jail.** City Manager Leif Ahnell said **she had called in sick that day.** The Boca City Council didn't have the authority to unseat the mayor. **Singer and council members Andrea O'Rourke and Monica Mayotte had all called for her resignation.** (Shatzman, 2018 – emphasis added)

There seemed to be a mad dash for the mayor's slot and one can only imagine why. But whatever the reason. The Council members weren't the only ones who piled on:

> Just days before her arrest, Haynie was reprimanded and fined $500 for similar infractions by the Palm Beach County Commission on Ethics. **She is still facing conflict-of-interest complaints filed with the state ethics commission.** (Shatzman, 2018)

And so it goes. A destination city with more than adequate tourist trade and the leadership still feels the need to pilfer funds and run game to make more money. A city with a nearly 10% poverty rate with a mayor that is stockpiling more than $300,000, along with her husband whose name in the charges is noticeably omitted.

We now go from the Deep South to the east coast.

Pittsburgh, (PA.) Mayor and "Developers for Dollars"

Whether the developers initiate the contact or the mayor's office does, the fact still remains that the developers play a major role in elections all over the country. Pittsburgh, Pennsylvania – the "Steel City" or "The City of Bridges" – is a metropolis with a population of 335,000, which makes it a city about the same size as Omaha only exponentially more famous and tourist-friendly. Pittsburgh may also be viewed as a "destination city" as opposed to the "fly over type" of city that Omaha is. Therefore it is most attractive to outsiders and as the relationship between developers and the mayoral position demonstrates, also quite attractive to "insiders" as well

An article by Rich Lord from the January 7, 2017 edition of the Pittsburgh Post-Gazette, titled, "Calls Turn Developers Into Donors for Peduto," offers background and context:

> **Pittsburgh's top development official has asked developers to contribute to Bill Peduto's campaign, in a series of calls the administration contends were devoid of deal-making, but which others said are at odds with the spirit of reform the mayor once championed**. Long a critic of what he called "the mentality of pay to play," Mr. Peduto is making a bid for a second term, with no announced challenger. **Like incumbents past, he has filled a campaign war chest in part by collecting from people who do business with the city**. (Lord, 2017 – emphasis added)

So we find another "convert" from the talk against "pay to play" to someone who is more than willing to play – as long as the money is right. Doing business with people who donate money is indeed, a form of "deal-making" and it has been taking place in American politics for centuries, as the scores of political "bosses" across the country clearly prove. From Boss Crump (Memphis), Boss Cox (Cincinnati) and Boss Pendergast (K.C.) to Tomm Dennison of Omaha, Daley of Chicago, Huey Long of Louisiana and Bilbo of Mississippi, political bosses and the corruption that followed is as big a part of American politics as the vote itself.

As far as Pittsburgh's tendencies are concerned,

> In October 2015, the mayor was joined in his fundraising calls by chief of staff Kevin Acklin, **who chairs the board of the Urban Redevelopment Authority**. Mr. Acklin said **that he took two half-days of vacation, during which he called 23 people and asked them to contribute.** URA records and city emails indicate that **at least 12 of the 23 people, or their firms, had business before the URA board in the**

> **year following the calls.** Mr. Acklin said the calls did not include conversation about any such business. (Lord, 2017 – emphasis added)

Bullshit. The calls were geared toward generating interest and locating donors, plain and simple. Peduto wanted a second term and was bound to get it and he knew that the best way to do so was to contact and corral the development community. Peduto won, and right after the inaugural he began laying out development-related ideas. According to a January 2, 2018 headline in Trib Total Media, "Pittsburgh Mayor Bill Peduto Wants to Focus on Development, Not Politics in 2nd Term." Doesn't that say it all?

More specifically, one of Peduto's development plans is, "providing housing for Pittsburgh's homeless. The mayor said he would like to model a program after one for homeless veterans in which the city, Allegheny County and nonprofits have provided housing within 90 days."   (Bauder, 2018)

Other changes Peduto sees coming:

> • Development of 700 acres of woodland in Hays into a "passive park" with about 10 percent of the land dedicated to housing. Peduto said city real estate taxes from any housing on the site would go toward providing universal preschool.

> • Development of a 13-acre former industrial property next to the North Shore's Rivers Casino. Washington County-based Millcraft Investments is planning a "nearly half-billion dollar" project that includes offices, housing, shops and a large Ferris wheel. Peduto is a fan of the Ferris wheel, which was invented in Pittsburgh.

> "Because of the way that the river is and the way that it juts out right by the West End Bridge, I think it would give a really unique view that few Pittsburghers have seen on the Golden Triangle," he said.

> • Development of an urban farm on the site of the former St. Clair Village.

> • Long awaited construction on the former Civic Arena property in the Lower Hill District.

> • Paving and infrastructure improvements on Carson Street through the South Side. (Bauder, 2018)

Now back to before his re-election and the money involved:

> Mr. Peduto said that it's natural that his right-hand man would help to raise campaign dollars. **"My chief of staff and I work together on a vision and an agenda and getting things done,"** he said. "It's good to know that he's one of the people that is **helping to make sure that we stay in office."** (Lord, 2017 – emphasis added)

And that is just what took place as we now know. There were some concerns, however:

> An official in a statewide reform advocacy group, though, said such calls put the recipients in a tough spot. **Anyone in Mr. Acklin's role "has life-or-death powers over the projects that these developers are pursuing,"** said Bob Warner, vice chair for issues at Common Cause PA. **"How is a developer supposed to feel? ...** I don't think any citizen should feel that **he's compelled to contribute to a particular politician to protect his business interests."** (Lord, 2017 – emphasis added)

Of course it's a matter of forcing a developer to "feel compelled" to contribute, to follow the leader, as it were. These white men know what time it is and they know that in order to "play the game" you have to get into the game. It's the same old "pay to play" that these people have been effectively operating behind closed doors for centuries. There are more "interests" to be protected than just "business interests," however:

> Mayors have traditionally appointed a top staff member to head the URA's five-member, volunteer board, but have taken varying stances on whether that person should have a political role. Tom Murphy, mayor from 1994 through 2005, said his top aide and URA chairman "Tom Cox clearly did not make calls. ... **You try to avoid the impression of cronyism or favoritism."** He said he has **"every reason to believe that Bill and his administration are very honest."** (Lord, 2017 – emphasis added)

Peduto and his administration "are very honest," huh? Why? Because you say so! What is honest about these white men and what they are willing to do to get elected and then stay in office? What is printed in the newspapers or broadcast over the airwaves is always only the tip of the political iceberg; the real dirt remains covered up unless the FBI gets involved. Pittsburgh is no exception – it's just that they haven't been caught yet.

> Mr. Peduto said the URA has taken **the same approach with all developers, whether they've supported his campaigns or not**. "This is a city that's open for business," he said, "not a city that's for sale." (Lord, 2017 – emphasis added)

What's the difference? If you're "open for business" that also includes monkey business! It means you can be "negotiated" with. It means that you are "open" to whatever is being offered. And that means that the city may not be "for sale," but it can sure in the hell be put up for rent or lease! Remember well that,

> A decade ago, as a councilman, Mr. Peduto prepared to challenge a sitting mayor. Luke Ravenstahl, though, raised seven times as much money, thanks to 10 five-figure contributions, **some from executives with city contracts, proposals or permit applications.** Mr. Peduto eventually quit the race. (Lord, 2017)

That means that Peduto learned a valuable lesson his first time around. And what do you think he did when he decided to run again? He used that same "get all the money you can" strategy that his former opponent had used!

Peduto acted as if he was doing the right thing when it came to controlling campaign contributions:

> **In 2008, Mr. Peduto called for campaign finance limits**. "Vendors, or potential vendors, believe [donating] is a requirement" for getting certain contracts, he said then. **"When you have the mentality of pay to play, you cannot have good government." His efforts led in 2009 to an ordinance limiting donations. Under a 2015 update**, candidates can't collect more than $2,700 per election from any individual, or more than $5,000 from any political action committee. (Lord, 2017 – emphasis added)

All that talk was a decade ago. That was then and this is now. People change over time. He won a mayoral election and wanted again. Maybe he sensed a closer contest this time around, forcing him to change his method of operation. While in office he met people, some powerfully rich people, people who made him promises and offered him guarantees. And this began to turn his head, make him re-think is previous position. This is politics and it tends to change you over time.

Now pay close attention to the following:

> As mayor, Mr. Peduto has raised funds from what he called "**one of the broadest bases of political support in all of Western Pennsylvania.** "We have a list of about a thousand people," he said. **Most of the outreach is done by professional fundraiser** Julie Hallinan, who has no government job. But reluctantly, the mayor has to make scores of calls himself. (Lord, 2017 – emphasis added)

Now we're talking about fundraising lists and "professional fundraisers." And that is where the talk about campaign finance reform begins to get swept under the rug. Once you start turning the fundraising over to people who raise funds for a living, then you are turning it over to people who will and can do whatever it takes to get their hands on those funds and funding commitments. This includes wining and dining, a budget for tickets to Steeler and Pirate games, and so on. Pittsburg is a destination city so luring people into the mayor's office for a one-on-one would be deemed an honor and a privilege. And once that's done and lunch is served (along with a little wine or beer), then out comes the checkbook. That's how it gets done.

More along those lines more can be gleaned from the following statements:

> **"While you have them on the phone, you have to get two things: an amount, and a date"** by which it will be paid, he said. "[I]t's like a fishing expedition where you hook the fish, **and you hand the rod over to your pro, who is Julie, and her job is to reel it in."** "And then there's a handful that are given out to a few people who do follow-up phone calls," he said. "Kevin's one of them." (Lord, 2017)

Peduto sounds like an idiot. To begin with, if you're fishing and you get a fish on the hook, you risk losing that fish if you hand that rod and reel over to someone else. I don't even fish and I know that much. Secondly, the key to the first statement is not getting an amount and a date: the key is how you got the phone number in the first place and in this day and age of "caller ID," if that person is going to pick that phone up. And THAT is when the real action begins because if they pick it up they've made a choice to engage in conversation.

Following is the key:

> In 2015, the mayor recounted, decisions on who called whom were made by asking, "Who feels comfortable calling this person?"Mr. Acklin provided the Post-Gazette with a list of the people he called. **Most are in the development business**. (Lord, 2017 – emphasis added)

And there's my argument. They have this list and Peduto admits that most of the people on it are developers. That means that this is a "selective list" made up of people who can do more than donate money. They are people who can be lured into making offers that will guarantee that an offer will be made! A developer is dependent on the city for its livelihood. The developer therefore has to curry favor. If a developer is on that list, then Peduto's people are doing that developer as big a favor as those developers will hopefully do for Peduto! It's not only quid pro quo (something for something) – it's also sine qua non – that which is absolutely essential.

And here's what we have to remember about that the Urban Redevelopment Authority that is in on this "arrangement" as well:

> The URA chairman makes no unilateral decisions, **but leads the mayor-appointed board that distributes millions in aid and buys and sells land.** There is no legal bar to his making campaign fundraising calls while off the clock and out of the office, **as long as contributions aren't traded for official decisions.** (Lord, 2017 – emphasis added)

How ludicrous. How are you going to know whether or not contributions are or are not "traded for official decisions"? Look at all the other mayors that were analyzed in this book who ended up going to jail and being kicked out of office because they thought that their "official decisions" would never be discovered after they accepted bribes.

But look at this hierarchy of fundraising. You have the URA chair who "leads" a mayor-appointed "committee" that gives out all those jobs that have to do with development and the issue of LAND. And how do you think this coterie makes that decision? It is clear that just as there is a fundraising list there is also a "list of priorities" and that is the list that determines who gets what and when they get it. It gets no more complex than that.

The art and key is to FAKE morality and above-the-board play, as is done in the following passage:

> **"Out of deep respect for the rule of law and ethics, at no time was any city or URA business discussed, nor were any requests for political support conditioned upon any express or implicit promises of any business with the city or URA,"** Mr. Acklin wrote in an email to the Post-Gazette. "I don't know that that's inappropriate," said Jim Ferlo, a URA board member and former state senator. "It's kind of clear why they're being called: They're unlikely to say no to a request." (Lord, 2017 – emphasis added)

What do you expect this guy Acklin to say or write? He's not going to issue a confession or admission that its pay for play. He's going to bring up ethics and the law as if they don't spend time working to circumvent both. If you want to deter criticism, just pretend that you have given some consideration to "ethics." That is what Omaha did when they formed this Omaha Business Ethics Alliance. After I wrote a major paper tearing them to shreds and sending it to the administrators charging that all of the 250 agencies that were members of it were in existence when racial segregation was and remains the law of the land. They did nothing.

Where were those "ethics"? They had no response. These ethics committees are no stronger than the people on them. And the people on them are regular white folks who could care less about including the variable of "race" in their racial decisions and considerations.

And just as I got no response from the vaunted Omaha Business Ethics Alliance leadership, the same appears to have happened to reporters in Pittsburgh, Pennsylvania:

> **None of the 23 people on Mr. Acklin's list who were reached by the Post-Gazette said they remembered getting a call from him requesting a donation.** But nearly all gave. The campaign logged personal checks from 18 of them, and got donations from employers, co-workers or PACs associated with the other five. During the last quarter of 2015, the 70 contributions associated with the people on the list exceeded $118,000, out of $627,000 the campaign raised that year. (Lord, 2017 – emphasis added)

All of the people gave, but "couldn't remember" if they got a call asking for the money? So that's where ethics always fall short. It's almost like pleading the Fifth Amendment, refusing to talk on grounds that may incriminate you. So they say "I can't remember," but the checks are the paper trail that shows what they did. If you want to get to the political facts, ethics be damned: follow the paper trail and follow the money.

One member of the city administration stated the obvious:

> City Controller Michael Lamb, a sometime rival of the mayor, called it **"very bad practice for the chairman of the board of the URA to be making political fundraising calls to the people the URA is intending to do business with. ... It makes the URA look like it's a pay-to-play organization."** (Lord, 2017 – emphasis added)

Of course it looks that way because that's the way it is! The thing that deflects even more criticism may be the name of the "department" itself. By naming it the "Urban Redevelopment Authority" it sounds like it is about making the city bigger and better, something that people in Pittsburgh have to agree with because their city is a marvel to behold. But what that department/committee actually DOES is defined based on political and economic need. And before you can get into the business or urban planning and development, you have to bring in the players who, in turn, are going to do their share to "pay to play." It's very simple and as Mr. Lamb said above, it is clear and apparent.

Note the dubious nature of the following attempt at an explanation:

> Mr. Peduto's backers have **in some cases won administration support,** but in other cases unsuccessfully pleaded their cases. For instance, Mr. Acklin said he called two top officials of Walnut Capital. **They donated $2,000 each, and also provided space, worth $1,000, for a campaign event. Weeks after the contributions,** Walnut sought URA backing to

> turn Shadyside's Hunt Armory into apartments. **The URA, though, chose a rival plan**. (Lord, 2017 – emphasis added)

"In some cases" the backers won administrative support. How about a list of the amounts doled out to that group and then the amount denied to the ones who were rejected? And let's put that selection of a rival plan in perspective. Just because the URA chose another plan other than the one that was submitted by a donor doesn't mean that some semblance of a compromise wasn't reached. I'm sure that the URA didn't just send a form letter saying "try again next year." Of course not. Walnut Capital was informed that they wouldn't be considered for this project, "but don't worry, we'll take care of you down the road." In my view the Walnut Creek application was not the final say, but that is what is implied by the previous excerpt.

The applicants on the "list" continues to be shared:

> Also on Mr. Acklin's call list was Chicago developer Dan McCaffery, who is **working with the city to redevelop the Strip District produce terminal.** He and his wife then **gave a combined $10,000 to the mayor's campaign.** Mr. McCaffery said that such a campaign solicitation is "nothing too unusual. **... I do development in three or four cities, and it's commonplace to support those who supported you."** Pittsburgh is **"not as demanding as some other places, really," he said, adding that the administration is "not a pushover."** (Lord, 2017 – emphasis added)

Let's break the previous information set down and make a clear distinction between outright pay to play and just a "regular donation" with no strings attached.

First off, McCaffery was already working with the city on a major project. So he was "on the inside" from the get-go, and who knows how many projects he had been "awarded" prior to that. In other words, he had a track record, and that is a powerful tool to have when you're bidding against high level developers who may have more capital than you. "Better the devil you know than the one you don't know."

Secondly, McCaffery and his wife gave $10,000 to the campaign knowing they would get that money back in future contracts. In other words there was no real "risk" involved; it was a short-term "investment" in the McCaffery future knowing that the projects they wanted would be awarded to them and as such, they would get their contribution back in spades.

Third, McCaffery claims to be doing business in "three or four cities" and that "it's commonplace to support those who supported you." This is the prototypical definition of quid pro quo. This is more of a guarantee that his

$10,000 donation was not wasted. A classic case of "I scratch your back, you scratch mine."

Fourth, Pittsburgh "is not as demanding" but it's also "not a pushover." Which one is it because it can't be both. It can be a hybrid of both. Pittsburgh may be "demanding" when in public view or on paper, but what takes place behind closed doors, especially with the kinds of advantages and guarantees that the McCaffrey's had to offer, can be viewed as a "pushover." As in "push over" that sofa pillow – there's a check for ten grand under it!

The URA appears to be the key to the allocation of assignments for the city of Pittsburgh. As Lord (2017) explains it,

> **The URA has supported a $7.5 million subsidy for street and utility improvements near the terminal, but hasn't yet gotten all of the other necessary approvals.** Also on Mr. Acklin's call list **was Trek Development president William Gatti, who donated $7,000 to Mr. Peduto's 2013 campaign, plus $3,000 in late 2015.** Mr. Gatti has **worked with the URA on projects** including The Bradberry building in Central Northside. (Lord, 2017 – emphasis added)

The URA is calling the shots in return for contributions to Peduto and his campaign slush fund. This is one more example of how these white men "get around" the rules and avoid public scrutiny. Pittsburgh didn't get to be a model city with so small a population without something under handed taking place behind closed doors. Their football team is called the Pittsburgh Steelers. Their government might want to be referred to as the Pittsburgh STEALERS.

The fix was in or, put another way,

> **Mr. Gatti said his firm is "enjoying a nice alignment with political leadership these days …** Mayor Peduto's platform, he's very interested in vital urban centers and affordability and historic restoration and many of our core values." **On Sept. 6, Mr. Acklin emailed Mr. Peduto, describing a proposed $2.15 million URA package to help Trek to convert The Bradberry into 16 apartments.** "That's $135K per unit, zero [rent] affordability," Mr. Acklin wrote. "I'm inclined to pull this from the [URA] agenda." (Lord, 2017 – emphasis added)

To begin with, how did Acklin get Peduto's email address. Was there no introductory memo or just a straightforward proposal to convert the apartments? Was a deal already in the making? It sounds as if the deal has already been approved, especially with Acklin having already run the numbers on how much the project will cost and possibly generate. There is no way he's going to "pull" a project from the agenda when so much work has been invested in it.

And by January of 2018 the Northside Chronicle reported that it was a done deal. According to the article by Jeff Geissler,

> This is a step forward for the Garden Theater Block, **where developers and their proposals have come and gone for almost 30 years**. Q Development and **Trek Development Group first partnered in 2014 when the Urban Redevelopment Authority of Pittsburgh requested proposals to develop the block.** The developers submitted plans to renovate the area, but **zoning disputes** in the area blocked their project ideas. (Geissler, 2018 – emphasis added).

It was clear that the project was going to go through because when there are so-called "Zoning issues" a "variance" can always be requested. If not that, which is usually issued at the state level, there are ways that the locals can go around changing and altering zones just as they do when they want to raze or invade a black community using Eminent Domain approaches.

Therefore,

> "When the full development proposal was overturned in the zoning court case, **the development team agreed to pursue just the Bradberry,**" said Rick Belloli, principal with Q Development. "We have a particular affinity for Frederick Osterling's work.**"Both firms hope to continue working with the city to renovate and develop that block**. "Currently, the URA (Urban Redevelopment Authority) still owns and controls the other five vacant buildings on the block as well as vacant lots, **and we continue to work with them on the future of that portion of the block**," Belloli said. (Geissler, 2018 – emphasis added)

So the original plan was altered in order to comply with zoning regulations. The incrementalist approach, which could not be done if those involved did not have a commitment that they would have the time and priority option to develop in the future. It's a long term deal that begins with short-term riches. And there is no doubt about it that the "development team," as it was called, is all white.

Moving on:

> **Mr. Peduto responded that he was "pretty sure it does include affordability."** Though there was actually **no guarantee of low-income units,** the package remained on the Sept. 8 agenda, and won initial approval. **Mr. Acklin said last week that he got "a verbal commitment" to "workforce" rents.** "I want that to be converted to something legally enforceable in the future," before the URA finalizes the package. (Lord, 2017 – emphasis added)

When it came down to the promise of "workforce rents" and "affordability, it was a token gesture at best. According to an article just over a year later, when the project was done, here is what was reported:

> They plan to open the four-story building in March, according to Rachel DeVemey, assistant property manager at Trek Development. The apartments will range in price from $993 to $2183 monthly. **"We have four two-bedroom units, and the rest are one-bedroom. And we do have four units that will be affordable housing,"** DeVemey said. (Beissler, 2018)

Four units out of sixteen will be deemed "affordable." I don't consider $993 to $2183 examples of "accordable housing." But those who made the decision didn't say "affordable to whom", and that is the catch. Men with this kind of access, these types of resources and power over the land can define things the way they choose, circumvent zoning laws and continue to lie to the public and still turn a profit. After all, their families and homes will be located nowhere NEAR the development zone.

Now we can return to the pre-development time of 2017:

> **In October, the Peduto administration announced that it was adopting the "P4 Performance Measures," making development decisions based on "people, planet, place and performance" — not politics**. The URA will "score every project," Mr. Acklin said, based on job creation, environmental impact, inclusiveness and public benefits. "If you're going to do development in the city, this is what we expect, in a very open and transparent manner." (Lord, 2017 – emphasis added)

The alliteration sounds nice and poetic but the fact is it's a bullshit cover-up. The attempt is to deflect attention from the "buddy system" that is taking place and making it appear to the voters as if Peduto is doing all the decision making and development-oriented business above board. The fact that the URA "scores every project" doesn't mean a damn thing unless you understand the quantitative basis behind the scoring system, what the scoring system represents and whether or not there are penalties involved. Again, it sounds good but it's all sound and fanciful musing minus substance and fulfillment.

Following is another way that attention can be diverted through unkept promises and bullshit tactics:

> **Mr. Peduto contends that the contribution limits are another brake on undue influence**, because five-figure donations are no longer allowed. The fundraising push in which Mr. Acklin participated, though, benefited from **a quirk of timing**. (Lord, 2017 – emphasis added)

Contribution limits don't mean anything when the quantity of the donation can be circumvented through a series of smaller sum donations. For instance, if I want to give ten grand, I might be stopped because of that large figure, but through the skillful abuse of shell companies and other "donor fronts," I can make ten donations of one thousand dollars apiece and end up with the same result.

There is no such thing as a "quirk of timing." But the skillful use of timing, through stall tactics and delays, can make everyday segments of reality appear to be "quirkish." All of this is a part of the political game that these white men play because they have no respect for the intellects of the voting public. Even under the guise of attempting to "clean things up" there are still gaps and holes that can restore the end result: business as usual.

For instance,

> In September 2015, Mr. Peduto's former aide, Councilman Dan Gilman, proposed a new campaign finance ordinance. It passed council on Oct. 20, 2015, **raising the limits on contributions by individuals to mayoral campaigns from $2,000 to $2,700 per election**. It disallowed **a practice called stacking, which had enabled contributors to give a candidate $4,000 at one time — $2,000 for the primary, and $2,000 for the general election. It took effect Nov. 4, 2015, the day after a general election**. (Lord, 2017 – emphasis added)

"Stacking" can be easily circumvented because it rests on the premise that those making contributions are going to be on the up-and-up. This is politics and the "hidden contribution" is the order of the day. In this case, you give two grand on the books and then meet at a secluded motor lodge over a few beers and give another four grand. Then a few weeks later at a private club you slip in another two grand then you wait to "post" the final two thousand dollar payment on the books following the election. That makes ten grand but only four thousand have been reported. You don't think these white people, skilled in the history of deception and lies, haven't figured that out yet?

Moving on and you get an idea of what I mean where "timing" is of the essence:

> **During the two weeks between the new law's passage and its effective date, Mr. Peduto's campaign collected $240,000, in part by collecting "stacked" donations of as much as $4,000 from 29 individuals or partnerships, and as much as $8,000 from three PACs**. After the new law reset the campaign finance game clock, they collected within weeks **additional checks from seven of those donors.** (Lord, 2017 – emphasis added)

And there you go. All those proposed bills, ordinances, amendments and various rules and regulations those are just a front and a façade in an effort to convince law enforcement and monitoring entities that "the record" has a concern about cheating. And that is true. But the concern is about protecting the cheaters, not bringing them to justice. Without any kind of rules in writing, that paves the way for closing down the system until written regulations can be implemented – not obeyed or followed, just implemented. This has been going on for a long time and these people are experts at it. In the final analysis, they are laws made by lawless men.

In addition to the "stacking" there is the issue of the "reset:"

> The combination of stacking and the reset allowed the McCaffery family, Highmark Health PAC and the International Brotherhood of Electrical Workers Local 5 to give $10,000 each in late 2015. From Mr. Acklin's list, a Walnut **partner's wife gave $6,700**, a CORE Realty executive contributed $6,666.67, and others pitched in between $3,000 and $5,000. (Lord, 2017)

You can donate through shell companies, the wives of the corporate leaders who may or may not use their maiden names, your children – there are a myriad of ways to get around these so called "campaign finance laws." Who better to break or violate them than the con men who created them?

Furthermore,

> Mr. Peduto said that his campaign fundraising effort has become so broad, **raising $3.3 million since 2012**, that even if checks from a firm add up to $10,000, no single contributor is more than "a drop in the bucket." **He said his method is less prone to abuse** than that of some past administrations, in which private, unofficial "bundlers" gathered checks, and expected favorable treatment in return. (Lord, 2017 – emphasis added)

Take notice that Peduto says that his method is "less prone to abuse," not immune from abuse or incapable of it. Being "less prone" to something means that an effect on it can still be made and in this case, that impact is in the millions of dollars, with more money waiting in the wings. In a destination city like Pittsburgh, the sky is the limit: those harbors, those bridges and all those natural resources, a skyline waiting to be expanded upon – Peduto and his cronies know they are sitting on a gold mine.

Put another way,

> **Acknowledging that city "history or tradition is all over the map on this,"** Mr. Murphy disputed any notion that local officials make decisions based on contributions. **"Rarely is there a quid pro quo that actually happens."** Mr. Ravenstahl, who also placed his chief of staff atop the URA board, could not be reached for comment. (Lord, 2017 – emphasis added)

The previous excerpt contains both bullshit and an outright lie. Let me elaborate.

In the former instance the issue of the "history or tradition" of the city being all over the map is a general truism. Each administration comes in with its own way of doing things, but the end result is the same: to stay in office for as long as you can, make money, change the skyline and work your way into the history books.

Next comes the outright lie wrapped in the claim that "Rarely is there a quid pro quo that actually happens." Who does this guy think he's bullshittin'? The fact of the matter is, quid pro quo is the order of the day. As they say on the streets, "you gotta bring ass to get ass." That means something for something. In Swahili it's "izandla ziyagezana", which translates to mean "one hand washes the other." So where does this guy get off denying what is obviously a universal and cross-cultural reality?

Winding down we find out exactly why Acklin is so busy and diligent and committed to his job. Take a look at his salary:

> Mr. Warner, of Common Cause, said true reform shouldn't include campaign calls from a top development official to developers. "As an architect of the city's campaign finance reform law, Mayor Peduto should certainly recognize the impropriety of this activity and stop it immediately." **Mr. Acklin, who earns $107,000 with the city**, said he didn't make fundraising calls in 2016. He didn't attend the mayor's Nov. 15 fundraiser, for which contributions should be disclosed Jan. 31. (Lord, 2017 – emphasis added)

Acklin had better hustle and do the job lest he lose that six-figure salary! He and Peduto are therefore joined at the hip, both working for the city and both committed to making sure that it stays that way. In vintage lap dog-master relations, it is clear who is calling the shots and who is the flunky. Bearing in mind that, "The hand that feeds controls," take note of the following:

> Mr. Peduto, though, **didn't rule out calling his chief of staff to the phone bank if he faces a challenger this year.** "It will be basically back into the war room, on the phone, making the phone calls, **raising the money, one by one, until we get to the point of around $2 million."** (Lord, 2017 – emphasis added)

So it becomes clear who is calling the shots and what Acklin's "real" role is with the City of Pittsburgh. The developer-mayor relationship is alive and well and living in the Steel City.

Salt Lake County (UT.) Mayor Meets With Developers

Another approach that is often used by mayors who may feel that their money is threatened is what I call "the fake town hall meeting" scam. The City of Omaha often uses it when they feel that they have to buttress their on-going leeching for Federal grant money for community projects, the police or some other local initiative. They hastily set up a meeting, prepare a power point presentation, answer as few questions as possible, and make sure that the constituents are out of town by sundown.

It appears that a similar concern for public anger took place in June of 2018 regarding a proposed "development." In a June 11th report that appeared under the headline, "Salt Lake County Mayor to Host Meeting Over Controversial Olympia Hills Development," , reporter Cristina Flores KUTV.com, we find the following brouhaha about to take place:

> (KUTV) -- **After receiving hundreds of complaints about a massive, proposed development** in the south part of the Salt Lake Valley, Salt Lake County **Mayor Ben McAdams is hosting a town hall meeting** … Residents and leaders in Herriman, Riverton and West Jordan met with McAdams on Monday, **as he holds the power to veto the county council's near unanimous approval of the project.** (Flores, 2018 – emphasis added)

Again, it's the mayor of the city that holds the ultimate veto power (in addition to the committee assignments and domination over various city department heads). The "town hall meeting" is a façade to respond to the more vocal residents. After he pacifies them, he will then move on and it will be business as usual.

Moreover,

> Residents, who want to block the current plans for the project, **recently filed paperwork to gather signatures and force the issue to the ballot.**They want the project scaled-down. "Hopefully we can avoid a showdown," said McAdams. The Olympia Hills project, would include **nearly 9,000 housing units, including single-family homes, apartments and town homes. It would make space for 33,000 new residents on 900 acres.** (Flores, 2018 – emphasis added)

It was a high density project and the residents didn't like the idea. McAdams wanted some kind of balance but ended up having to veto the plan. He hosted the community meeting in early June and by mid-month had made his decision. This was one of those "planned communities" which means it was lily-white and didn't include any affordable housing. But the residents knew that with high population density comes conflict – they should know since that is what they do to black and brown people when they want to segregate and isolate them into small ghetto/barrio areas. As with most cases involving these developers and mayors, the variable of "race" is always a factor.

Continuing:

> Salt Lake County Councilman Jim Bradley, who voted in favor of the development said it will also include space for a satellite campus for Utah State University, shops and work spaces. Unlike the concerned residents, who say the plan was rushed-through and is too much for the currently over-crowded roads and schools to handle, Bradley said the development was well thought-out. "This didn't happen overnight," he said. (Flores, 2018)

I believe McAdams is lying. When cowardly white men want to get a project underway, they rush it through. They do that so that the community's more radical element, which includes people of color, won't have time to respond to what is taking place. While it may be true that it didn't happen overnight as far as the whites-oriented "planning" component, there can be no doubt that the exposure to what was going to take place was thrust upon residents with the quickness.

The key word is density and when that word appears white folks know what can happen. The reasons used are infrastructure strain: on the roads, sewers and the like. But socially speaking, we know what the real fear is: "the niggers are coming"! And that would run counter to the whole purpose of a "planned community." The "plan" is to get as far out, yet as close to freeways and transportation back into town, as possible.

Therefore,

> While Bradley acknowledges the project is really big, **he said a high-density development is a necessary solution to the fast growing**

> **population in the Salt Lake Valley which is supposed to grow by
> 200,00 over the next 10 years.** Most of that growth he said, will be in
> the southwest part of the Salt Lake Valley and those new residents will
> need places to live. "It's a finite valley. **You've only got so much land
> and it's going very rapidly,"** said Bradley. (Flores, 2018 – emphasis
> added)

Finite valley. Limited land. That doesn't' stop these white people when they want to segregate. But in this case they know that with that anticipated growth in population is also going to come a demographic transition, increasing numbers of brown and black people who will be able to afford to move into those "planned areas." And that is going to scare white people because in the presence of equitable living conditions, the myth of white supremacy can easily be exposed for the sham that it is. You can see their flaws, hear their arguments, watch the police getting called, see how sluttish their women are and are much alcohol and drugs are consumed behind the safe gates of those "planned communities." These are the communities where the cops, the reporters and the decision makers live. So they surely don't want any "witnesses of color" seeing them for what they really are.

> He said the county council spent a lot of time considering the plans by
> developer Doug Young before taking two votes to approve re-zoning to
> make it happen. Bradley said all along the plan has been **to build it
> phases, over decades, so as to allow infrastructure to catch up with
> building.** (Flores, 2018 – emphasis added)

The incrementalist approach, allowing infrastructure to catch up with building is only one part of the issue. The main part is the people moving n catching up with the infrastructure! The more people, the more toilets that are flushed, showers used, lawns watered and driveways to be parked in. These white people cannot deal with equitable relations with people who do not look like they look. For instance white people have to tan and sit in the sun to look the way black and brown people look naturally. Then, when the brown and black people don't have to bother with it, they (whites) become envious and begin asking stupid questions and doing what they can to promote whatever "advantages" there are that come along with being "pale," "fair," "light-skinned" and so on.

> He said at no time, did the council consider **pushing through a plan
> without considerations for upgrading the water and sewer system as
> well as adding roads and more options for transit**. "If people knew
> how it was going to look, they'd be comfortable with that I'm quite
> certain," he said. (Flores, 2018 – emphasis added)

All this is fine and good and easy to say "after the fact." But the plan was being considered, was it not? Somebody was pushing. Not because it got stopped doesn't negate the fact that bad intentions were at the source of the plan being considered from the get-go. These white people are not afraid to "go ahead and build" and then deal with infrastructure at a later date, as the need presents itself. This goes on all the time in communities that want to expand and gain more numbers so that they will qualify for more Federal aid.

McAdams is no saint with his veto – he had ulterior motives as well, as the following excerpt bears out:

> Utah Congresswoman Mia Love said on Twitter that Ben McAdams, who is running for her seat, **accepted $10,000 in campaign contributions from the Olympia Hills developers**. She said Salt Lake County mayors concerned about the project **reached out to her and she said in the tweet that "McAdams is trying to look like a power broker following outrage w/the Olympia project."** "Utahns won't be fooled w/"pay McAdams to play" tactics," she said in that tweet. (Flores, 2018 – emphasis added)

It should be known that Mia Love is a black woman. Remember I told you that somewhere down the line the variable of "race" is going to play an increasingly significant role in mayoral elections and developer relationships all over America. McAdams plans to run against her which is why he didn't want to piss off potential voters over some land issue. He is seeking a seat in Congress and so far he appears to be raising some major money. As it was reported in the *Salt Lake Tribune,*

> Heading into the homestretch of their close 4th District congressional race, GOP Rep. Mia Love and Democratic Salt Lake County Mayor are essentially tied in the amount of cash they have amassed. Both have $1.2 million in the bank, according to new quarterly campaign finance disclosure forms — although McAdams has a slim $15,880 more. (Davidson, 2018)

Look at all the money involved in this small community and its development concerns. These two politicians are rooted in the development world and they are raising and spending millions of dollars. Check it out:

> While they have the same amount of cash now, Love has been raising and spending significantly more. **She took in $1.02 million in the past quarter and spent $722,000. During this two-year election cycle, she has amassed $3.3 million and spent $2.6 million.** McAdams gathered $620,000 during the quarter and spent $235,000. **He has raised $1.7**

> **million since he entered the campaign last October and spent
> $428,000.** (Davidson, 2018 – emphasis added)

What??! And the city is so insignificant in the face of the multi millions spent elsewhere that the millions spent in Salt Lake don't even seem to register. And yet the money is calling the shots and land is being moved and buildings constructed and skylines altered. It all fits together.

Another aspects worthy of consideration is the mudslinging and name calling that usually comes along with such fierce competition and with such enormous sums of money being raised and spent:

> "During her time in Congress, Rep. Love has blown the federal deficit up into the stratosphere — and her campaign report shows she can't seem to stop spending, no matter where she goes," McAdams said. "She spends it nearly as fast as she raises it, which shows her true lack of fiscal conservatism." (Davidson, 2018)

Not to be outdone, Love has a counter-argument:

> Love, meanwhile, said her outraising McAdams shows that voters have more trust in her. "Between Ben's recent gaffe with the massive high-density Olympia Hills development near the Herriman area, his extensive employment history with Hillary and Bill Clinton, his wishy-washy rhetoric regarding abortion and the fact he doesn't even live in the 4th district, voters are realizing Ben just isn't someone they can trust." **The two-term congresswoman** had recently attacked McAdams for taking $10,000 in donations from Olympia Hills developers, but that was before he vetoed the County Council's approval of the controversial project — saying it was too dense. (Davidson, 2018)

McAdams wants to move up the political ladder and Love wants to keep her job in Congress. Both are beholden to developers, although McAdams does not even live in the district – which is quite legal in Utah.

Newark, (NJ) Mayor, Developers, and Affordable Housing

Sometimes social concerns do win out. When that happens developers take off their hats of greed and don their "caps of compassion" – or at least feigned compassion. Such is the case in Newark where the issue is developers as they relate to "affordable housing."

The mayor of that city, Ras J. Baraka, actually created a position to make sure that residents had access to affordable housing "opportunities." As one article from the City of Newark explained it:

> Mayor Ras J. Baraka announced today that the city is **advertising to fill the position of Affordable Housing Manager,** a post created to ensure that Newark residents have access to the city's **growing number of affordable apartments and homes and that developers comply with the City's new and existing affordable housing laws.** The Affordable Housing Manager will lead the mayor's initiative to **create and preserve affordable homes and apartments in all of the city's neighborhoods.** (City of Newark, 2017 – emphasis added)

There is no doubt that this housing will be in the older parts of the city with emphasis on the black community. When these mayors say "affordable housing" they are talking about a form of "redlining" that means placing poor people in areas where there are other poor people. By having such a "manager," incoming poor people – immigrants, minorities, single parents – can therefore be "steered" to this housing without the actions appearing to be rooted in class segregation.

The article informs us that,

> "The availability of affordable housing in Newark is growing **fueled by new laws mandating that future development include housing that residents can afford.** This is an important element of our strategy to ensure that all residents have the opportunity to benefit from the city's surge of development and increasing prosperity. **We are conducting a search to find someone who will connect residents with available affordable housing and ensure that developers comply with our affordable housing requirements." Mayor Baraka said.** (City of Newark, 2017 – emphasis added)

Those laws are not "new" – not as far as the Federal government is concerned. Before these white developers can put up those multi-unit dwellings, there is a Federal requirement that a certain percentage be earmarked as "affordable." That is what happened in the case of Trek Development in the city of Pittsburgh, remember? Recall that it was a four story building and that a certain percentage had to be deemed affordable, consisting of "workforce rents.

Take note of the job duties for this proposed "Affordable Housing Manager." His duties are, quite simply, "steering" people. This is what the white man did when black people migrated North from the Deep South. The white real estate people came in and "directed" them to the areas where "you can be around your own kind" and "you will feel more comfortable" and "you will be able to afford to live here." That was the line that was used then, and evidently it is still being used in a city like Newark, a city that is 53.4%African-American and 29% Latino. And according to the City-Data.com website Newark, a city of 273,546 also had a poverty rate of 37% in 2016. So it's poor and minority and the need for affordable housing assures that there will be no "inter-mixing" between those who are white and those who are "non-white."

The mayor is black and in fact when he won re-election in 2018 he brought in Johnny Gill and Danny Glover. But just because the mayor is a man of color doesn't mean that the "program" is going to be pro-black. The program, regardless of the race of the head honcho, is going to be pro-business and pro-development. After all, that affordlabe housing has to be renovated and built by somebody.

The new position that Baraka will create is an interesting one, According to the City of Newark website,

> **This position will be a senior-level executive role which will immediately coordinate the implementation of the Mayor's Inclusionary Zoning Program** and neighborhood housing preservation programs, develop a strategic approach to **promoting housing for seniors and protected groups (LGBTQ, homeless and disabled);** and propose innovative ways to engage Newark residents and interest groups to explore housing needs and opportunities. (City of Newark, 2017) (emphasis added)

Notice that people of color as a minority group, are not mentioned. That is because people of color are low-income, and as stated elsewhere in this book, the white man reserves the power of selective definition and defines "affordable housing" in different ways based upon whatever the need is at the time. In an area of millionaires, affordable housing is all housing; in a city with a 40% poverty rate like Newark, affordable housing is based on what the income of a given area is. With the middle class being moved to an outward ring, those who are low income are concentrated in certain "pockets of poverty," as they are called by the Department of Housing and Urban Development. Therefore what is affordable in those pockets is actually more like public or low-income housing.

So the Affordable Housing Manager is not about locating housing for the poor because that is what the public housing around the city is for. Alder Creek is the newest public housing facility with Newark having torn down four high rises in recent years. Total low income apartments in Newark - (21,419); Total rent assisted apartments (17,346) and the shortage of Affordable apartment properties, a scant 157, paving the way for the revived interest in a city where 78% of housing is occupied by renters.

Specifically, what will be the duties of this newly created position? According to the City of Newark website the new manager will be:

- Making Newark residents aware of **the range of affordable housing opportunities.**
- Creating, maintaining and publicizing a central directory/office/website **where residents can apply for affordable housing units** or be directed to where to apply.
- Ensuring that Newark residents receive the preferences in rental decisions to which they are entitled
- Monitor the **compliance by developers** of the City's affordable housing mandates.
- Ensuring compliance with all City **affordable housing mandates and covenants.**
- Overseeing the development and implementation of a 5-year Affordable Housing Compliance and Management Plan.
- **Ensuring resident and community involvement** in policy development. (City of Newark, 2017 – emphasis added)

The compliance by developers could well be the key if the other cities in this book are any indicator. The shortage of affordable housing (see the earlier numbers) is of paramount importance in Newark. As the city's own website makes clear, "Affordable housing has been a major priority for the Baraka administration since taking office in 2014. The Housing Inclusion Ordinance, one of the strongest in the nation, mandates that **developers that build or rehabilitate a development of more than 30 units must set aside 20 percent as affordable housing"** (City of Newark, 2017 – emphasis added)

The developers will get more work but they will be monitored. But if we have learned anything about mayors in these cities, the monitoring will be selective. The creation of an Affordable Housing Manager, a member of the executive staff, will mean that the position is under the thumb of the mayor's office. And "the hand that feeds, controls."

But there are incentives for developers as well:

> **A parallel ordinance requires that all developers receiving tax abatements must include affordable housing.** The City's efforts to expand and preserve affordability include the sale of **city-owned plots of land to potential homeowners**, financial and other help for residents interested in home buying, **helping small contractors to grow and develop housing around the city,** and programs to help homeowners with underwater mortgages to avoid foreclosure. (City of Newark, 2017) (emphasis added)

Developers again are a key part of the mayoral decision making in a city, even one as rife with poverty as Newark.

Plano (TX.) Mayor Bankrolled by Developers

Despite his rather anglicized name Plano Mayor Harry LaRosiliere is another African-American mayor. But unlike Baraka, he is the leader of one of the richest cities (per capita) in America. When you find a black mayor that is elected by well-do-do white people it should be clear that you've got an Uncle Tom on your hands. White people do not elect militant black men or women to manage their city and their money. Before serving the two terms as mayor he was on the common council for two terms. The claim is that Plano is "45% non-white," but you couldn't tell it by taking a drive through it: this town is as white as they come except maybe for some people of color crammed into some of the apartment complexes that align the main drive, Preston Road.

The fact is, LaRosiliere is a Haitian immigrant so that explains it. He was raised in Harlem and has moved Plano from a bedroom community to being a suburb of Dallas. That means he's connected with some of those corporations that he's brought into Plano, including Morgan Chase and Company, Boeing, Toyota, the FedEx office, and Liberty Mutual Insurance, not t mention Ross Perot's already mega-rich

Developers shaped the mayor's position in this rich city. I lived in nearby Cedar Hill, Texas for six years and worked in Plano as the director of the so-called Plano African-American Museum. I would alter find out that the museum, like most anything that has to do with black culture, is a sham and a façade. That's how a black man named LaRosiliere can become mayor and, as of 2017 won a second term. His platform: keep Plano suburban. In simple terms, keep it as lily-white has it has historically been.

In few places is the developer-mayor relationship more dominant and prominent than in Plano, Texas. Before getting into some background, note the fact that special interests were involved and all of them wanted to keep high density and apartments as far away from Plano as possible

The re-election was therefore clear enough was reported:

> Plano Mayor Harry LaRosiliere won a second term over three challengers, barely avoiding a runoff with Lily Bao, **who campaigned for change with the backing of a group called Plano Future.** "What the voters told us is that the politics of hope and vision is better than divisiveness and despair," LaRosiliere said late Saturday. "I'm always ready to listen and do what's best for our city. **But I'm going to do it in a manner that's going to unite the city, not divide us."**
> (Wigglesworth, 2017 – emphasis added)

LaRosiliere appeals to white folks, but one thing I give him credit for: he has a beautiful black family, including two fine daughters. He seems to be doing everything right, but the fact is he's a mayor of a city that was formerly one of the most racist in the Dallas area. And it's still going on despite the presence of a black mayor. According to the January 25, 2018 issue of the Dallas News,

> Four black construction workers say they were subjected to racial harassment and discrimination while working on the new JPMorgan Chase regional office in Plano's Legacy West. Dallas-based Beck Co. is among the companies named in the lawsuit filed by Scott Perez LLP on behalf of the four workers: Lerone Boyd, Michael Marshall, Jimmy Allen, and Trojuan Cornett. (Halkias, 2018)

As those of you who are not black or Latino know, this is but the tip of the iceberg. Numerous cases like this take place in cities like Plano and little is ever done because it's considered par for the course. The story adds that,

> After the workers complained about the harassment to Beck, **the general contractor of the site, they were fired**, according to the lawsuit that was filed Tuesday in the 95th Judicial District Court of Dallas County. They said they also complained about the harassment to Aerotek, Inc., a staffing company on the project, and JR Butler, Inc., a crane operator at the site, **and nothing was done**. (Halkias, 2018 – emphasis added)

This is what "Plano Future" truly means. They are developing a cultural arts district (mimicking Dallas) and while the mayor might be well-meaning, the white man's definition of culture is different than the way black folks view it – just like that fake-ass Plano African American museum was nothing more than a "grant magnet" to attract cultural arts dollars to a building that was nothing more than a shack on stilts. I know because I was hired to "re-write and submit" the grant for future funding and was paid to do so. After I did it, I was summarily fired – just like the bruthas in the example. Only in my case it was done by black lesbians.

So how does a black man, married to a beautiful black woman, end up serving as a two term mayor of one of the wealthiest cities in America? Well remember the slogan, Plano Future? That's the key. That means curbing the number of poor and minority people who come into the city to live. That means controlling the population density or, as one article explained it:

> Two other city council candidates backed by Plano Future are headed to runoffs on June 10 while the fourth candidate supported by the group lost in a close race in Place 4. Plano Future focused its campaign on **curbing**

**the high-density apartments planned for the city and pledged to keep
Plano suburban** (Wigglesworth, 2017 emphasis added)

So the future is focused on curbing apartments and keeping Plano suburban.
That means white. And that is the vibe you get when you exit that DART train in
that city, which is but three blocks from the so-called Plano African-American
Museum.

With the goal and vision made crystal clear, let's look at the role that the
developers played in electing this black man for two terms. I think the headline of
an April 27, 2017 just about says it all, The article, written by Ross Kecseg is
titled, "Plano Mayor Bankrolled by Special Interests, Raises Ethical Questions."
What "ethics"? These white people use those ethics committees and ethics
organizations (Omaha's version) as a façade to deflect criticism from outside of the
city's boundaries. More likely than not everyone that is a member of that
committee is unethical because they are appointed by unethical people, just as
every member organization of the Omaha Business Ethics group was and remains
a part of the racial discrimination and non-hiring of blacks. That is about as far as
"ethics" are concerned (see the article on the Los Angeles Ethnics committee
elsewhere in this book).

The article begins:

> **Not only is Plano Mayor LaRosiliere backed by developers**, he's
> misled the Dallas Morning Citizens from one of Dallas' largest suburbs
> are **working hard to oppose their Mayor and his allies who've
> pushed for high-density developments despite overwhelming
> opposition from citizens.** Campaign finance records reveal the mayor's
> motive to ignore constituents: **local developers are largely bankrolling
> his reelection effort.** (Kecseg, 2017 – emphasis added)

You see: a black mayor is a mayor in name only. When white people elect a
black man to run a city you better believe that he's going to be more than just
"beholden" to that constituency: he is going to be RULED by them. The
developers are calling the shots and the call for high density developments means
apartments and condos. Plano will still be a wealthy city, but the developments will
qualify certain sections for Federal aid of some kind. And these dwellings will be
in the same general area to ensure that the poor people and the black people don't
interact with the "normal" folk. Feel me?

This black man won a second term in a city that is known for its racist ways
and history. According to one report,

Follow the Money

> Plano Mayor Harry LaRosiliere misled the *Dallas Morning News* when asked about his fundraising. **He suggested he'd raised only $60,000,** but that amount is what he raised since his last report. **It excludes tens of thousands in prior contributions he's used this election cycle.**(Kecseg, 2017 - emphasis added)

The white folks are calling the shots and LaRosiliere is just the puppet. As pointed out elsewhere in this book, these people know how to hide and camouflage donations and contributions, and they do it well. Supporting high density means more work for the developers because those developments mean more apartment buildings, more condos, more materials and more man-hours for each project.

According to one report,

> His campaign is also misleading voters with mailers claiming he's for "Suburban Quality of Life." **The Mayor has been one of the most vocal supporters of high density.** While he's raised traditional donations, **half of the $135,000 in contributions in 2016 came from individuals with direct ties to developers or their financiers.** They include PACs, executives, and individuals. (Kecseg, 2017 – emphasis added)

And so it goes: LaRosiliere rakes in the money in exchange for providing long-term development jobs for the white companies who, in turn, say nothing when the media comes snooping around asking questions. And we're not talking about a couple of apartment complexes, either. Check it out:

> **Mayor LaRosiliere's Unpopular High-Density Development Agenda**
> The donations shed light on why the LaRosiliere coalition has **relentlessly pushed for tens of thousands of new apartment units amidst vocal citizen opposition.** But it gets worse. He's also under fire for doling out tax dollars for costs the private developers should be paying. Below is the city's development plan, known as **the "Plano Tomorrow Plan."** Areas circled in red by Plano Future – a group of citizens opposed to the plan – indicate areas targeted for high-density. (Kecseg, 2017 – emphasis added)

An increase in population generates attention of the people at the Federal level to provide funding for cities based on their size. As Plano grows, so will the city's coffers. The key is to have a "vetting system" in place so that the people moving into those apartments are "acceptable" by white standards. That means well-to-do immigrants, middle and upper class minorities and others who aspire to the white way of life. These developments will more than likely be "communities of interest" or what they call "planned communities." Many will be gated.

Continuing:

> The mayor's coalition has pushed an unpopular density policy that aims **to urbanize the suburb at the behest of developers**, despite near-unanimous opposition from homeowners. **Critics argue thousands of additional apartments will further crowd Plano schools and exacerbate already dreadful traffic congestion.** They also claim the council **is improperly subsidizing developers**. Plano taxpayers are rightfully outraged the city is effectively diverting existing tax dollars away from improving major road arteries elsewhere. (Kecseg, 2017 – emphasis added)

Those taxpayers don't have a clue as to what is taking place. The mayor is not the major or lone decision maker in that city. As we have seen in other cities all over America, the mayor is beholden to developers and other corporate types, all committed to building office spaces, malls and altering the skyline. This obsession with building means that money can be used to "buy" political backing and with that backing goes the future direction of the city – *any city*.

Moving on:

> High-Density Stresses Budget for City Services
> Excessive high-density development increases total tax revenue, but decreases revenue *per resident*. This creates the false need for city officials to increase property tax burdens year over year – despite bragging about their "low" tax *rates* – and helps officials justify a May bond proposition that asks taxpayers to pay even more for needed infrastructure. **Meanwhile, big corporations moving to the area have been handed preferential tax breaks.** (Kecseg, 2017 – emphasis added)

Those big corporations are bringing jobs with them so that will shut up most of the citizens. Those corporations also wield a lot of power when it comes to needing housing for the influx of employees, many of whom are six-figure salary types who are not looking for any "apartment," but a high-end condo or a home in a gated community – all of which the developers can provide to them.

As the article makes clear,

> Stated differently, **the city gives new companies preferential treatment, while raising property tax burdens on everyone else**, and then asks taxpayers to pay even more in debt for core needs – **all while handing developers subsidies they don't need for projects Plano taxpayers oppose.** Kecseg, 2017 – emphasis added)

This is the formula and Plano residents better get used to it. The corporations that dominate Plano's economy are footing the bills for the rich employees who are going to buy houses and rent condos. They are then going to create a need for even more housing and that is where the developers come in and where the mayor lobbies to make Plano a "Dallas suburb." By linking itself to Dallas, Plano expands its tourism influence and can lure more people to the city since the Dallas Area Rapid Transit has a stop right there in midtown Plano. If the taxpayers get stuck for the tab, that's just the way it goes. Read about the other cities in this book and you'll understand the impact of the developer-mayoral power relationship.

San Diego, (CA.) Mayor's Aide Married at Developer's Estate

The expansive power of developers just keeps on coming. In San Diego it may have literally become a "family affair." In an article titled, "Mayor's Top Aide Got Married at Bayfront Estate of Developer and SoccerCity Supporter." In May of 2017 the San Diego Union Tribune reported what took place.

According to the article:

> "This rises to a level of sketchiness that I would be worried about."
> Months before he began meeting with promoters of the SoccerCity plan
> for the city-owned Qualcomm Stadium property, **Mayor Kevin
> Faulconer's right-hand man got married in a wedding and reception
> at the bayfront estate of a key player in the proposal.Stephen Puetz,
> chief of staff since Faulconer took office in 2014, took his vows at a
> private home across from Shelter Island owned by San Diego
> developer Morgan Dene Oliver.** (McDonald, 2017 – emphasis added)

Developers have different ways of influencing the city's decision makers. And then once it takes place, the collective lies can defend even the most misfeasant of actions. For instance,

> Puetz said he received no special treatment from Oliver. As soon as he
> was offered use of the estate, he said, he contacted the city Ethics
> Commission to see how he could best meet the conflict-of-interest rules.
> (McDonald, 2017)

Again remember that these ethics committee usually contain a few members whose concept of morality revolves around what are called "situational ethics." That means that their moral compass is on-again, off-again. They change with the wind and they can be bribed and they can be duped into accepting some of the most ludicrous arguments you will ever hear. Therefore contacting this "Commission" means nothing if the people on it are in the hip pocket of the mayor.

Furthermore,

> Puetz said he and his wife, former council aide and registered lobbyist
> Diana Palacios, paid for the wedding themselves, including a reasonable
> fee to Oliver for use of the property."I consider him a friend and a
> mentor," Puetz told U-T Watchdog. "He offered to let us use his house in
> Point Loma for the wedding as long as we paid for everything in full,
> which is very important to me and to my wife." (McDonald, 2017)

But why Oliver's house? If it wasn't a matter of money, why not go public? Why not rent a palatial estate someplace else? Why just so happen to get married at a house where a developer that you know and have done business with just so happens to reside? This is clearly a conflict of interest any way you cut it. It would be different if the developer were related to Oliver. But not like this. This is nothing short of an "in-kind gift" and it is clear that's what it is – a political "favor" that will be collected upon later on.

The article further informs us that,

> The wedding was held Aug. 15, 2015 — four months before Puetz,
> Faulconer and others began scheduling meetings with Oliver and
> SoccerCity investors. The first meeting was held over a Jan. 5, 2016,
> lunch at the downtown office of Oliver's development firm,
> OliverMcMillan. They have continued into this year as the project moves
> forward. (McDonald, 2017)

Come on, man! Only white people could get away with this degree of criminality and graft – illegally gotten gains. His main man gets married and then a few months later they do business with the power broker developer whose houses that guy got married in? is there no bottom? We're talking big money – paying a rent to get married is a pittance compared to the money involved in that development project. Check it out:

> **SoccerCity is a $1 billion redevelopment blueprint for the
> Qualcomm Stadium site vacated by the San Diego Chargers' move
> to Los Angeles in January**. At least two rival developers have raised
> questions about the plan's environmental impacts and permitting
> process. (McDonald, 2017 – emphasis added)

In other words this plan was long in the making because the San Diego Chargers' move to L.A. was a long time in coming and, in fact, the NFL was beginning to complain about how long it was taking. The fix was in as the following excerpt makes most clear:

> Faulconer called for the special election and supports the SoccerCity
> proposal. Oliver, a longtime Faulconer supporter, did not return a call
> seeking comment about the wedding or his role in SoccerCity. The
> Mayor's Office said Oliver is no longer involved in the redevelopment
> plan. If the City Council agrees to the election, voters will decide in
> November whether to grant the investors a 99-year lease allowing them
> to develop the Major League Soccer arena and thousands of homes and
> millions of square feet of commercial space on the public land.
> (McDonald, 2017)

As of a month before the election (when this book went to press), the mayor was going soft on the project, as was its largest backer, San Diego Padres partner Pete Seidler. According to the *San Diego Union-Tribune*, politics reigned supreme:

> There's another dynamic at play: Many of the principals of FS Investors
> are viewed as outsiders to the San Diego establishment while Friends of
> SDSU is populated with well-known, politically influential figures. With
> institutional support growing for the university-backed plan, **SoccerCity
> advocates have complained that the system is rigged**. (Smolens, 2018
> – emphasis added)

Of course it's rigged. To begin with Oliver is a very wealthy man. Check it out for yourself:

> **Oliver's 6,500-square-foot home features a private dock and
> sweeping views of San Diego Bay. The 4-bedroom, 6-bath house was
> recently on the market for $8.9 million**, according to real estate
> websites that now list the property as a pending sale.Puetz paid $427.23
> for use of the venue and $340 for a post-event cleaning … The rental
> cost was calculated as 1/30th of what a leading real estate website
> suggested the retreat would rent for by the month. (McDonald, 2017 –
> emphasis added)

These white men have been doing this since the early days of urban planning. They sit in these rooms and will even go so far as to "pretend" as if they are on opposite sides in an attempt to make the public think that there is an "ethical controversy." And the public can see it and they still don't do anything because it's white on white. It's about race as I've been trying to make clear. Even in a lily-white hick town, as some of the cities in this analysis have been, there is always a class element and if that is the case, then "race" is not far behind.

Skipping past the marriage costs, let's get to the gist of the developer-mayor relationship:

> **Ethics experts said public officials have a special responsibility to avoid appearances that they could gain personal benefit from their public service**. Adam Swenson, director of the Center for Ethics and Values at California State University Northridge, said accepting an offer of a constituent's private home for a personal event may not be the most prudent decision."It's not enough to be impartial, you have to be seen as impartial," he said. "You have to go the extra mile. This rises to a level of sketchiness that I would be worried about. Most of us can't go out and rent a multimillion-dollar house for a few hundred bucks." (McDonald, 2017)

The first line of the previous paragraph says it all: "avoid appearances that they could gain personal benefits from their public service." Everybody in this story was in violation of this basic edict. They didn't give a shit about any ethical considerations or the public – they did what they wanted to do and said "let the flak fall where it may." The money was there to be made and everyone involved was going to do what had to be done to set the table. It's very simple.

Want proof? Let us skip ahead past the ethics center's that the writer of this article foolishly consulted as if there was a true issue of "ethics" involved. Check out the preparation by the soon-to-be bride:

> A few months before the 2015 wedding, Diana Palacios left her position working for Councilman Scott Sherman and **accepted a job with Southwest Strategies, a public affairs and lobbying firm** … City disclosure reports show Southwest principals **regularly lobbied Palacios before they hired her.** After the wedding, Diana Puetz directly lobbied her husband and others in the Mayor's Office on behalf of six different clients, including the San Diego Padres. (McDonald, 2017 – emphasis added)

Behind closed doors. Resignations and then immediate re-hires in an economy where people far more qualified than Ms. Palacios are begging and applying job jobs? The fix was in. We'll see if the developer and his cohorts get their way.

Irvine, (CA.) Mayor Speaks of Importance of Development

Key developments and doing business with developers can sometimes be two totally different things. Following the "state of the city" address by Irvine mayor Don Wagner as he began his second term, the local newspaper, the Orange County Register reviewed and analyzed it and I will do the same to what they did, with emphasis on the role of "development." In fact, the reporter, Shimura

Shimura's March 2, 2018 article is headlined, "Here's What You Need To Know About Irvine Mayor's 2018 State of the City Address."

Based on my research, Irvine had been one of the safest cities for at over a decade. Yet Wagner reported it as if he deserved the credit:

> IRVINE – Don Wagner gave his second State of the City address as mayor on Tuesday, Feb. 27.Although the speech lacked any surprises or big announcements, it highlighted key developments and issues facing the city. Here's a summary. (Shimura, 2018). **Wagner said Irvine remains America's safety city for its size based on FBI statistics**. The Register's reporting also showed the chances of Irvine residents becoming a crime victim in recent years are lower than ever, despite some residents feeling otherwise. That's consistent with declining crime rates nationwide since the early 1990s. (Shimura, 2018 – emphasis added)

Irvine is one of those corporatist cities that is upper class and therefore people who don't have much money cannot afford to live there. According to my research, Irvine does a lot of international business and in fact, that is one of its goals. They built around the University of California and as a result, attracted the "kinds" of people that they wanted. According to the City of Irvine website, the population as of 2015 is 250,384, 45.7% of whom are white. The population is 38.2% Asian and 10% Hispanic. Irvine is only 1.7% African-American.

A whopping 65% of the population are college graduates and the median income is $92,663 a year. This is an upper class city, meaning few if any liquor stores or night clubs. The crime is limited to pranks by college students and as Wheeler & Shimura point out, "Because of the large number of corporations, the median income is high, but the other demographic realities also tell a story:

> Master-planned around the then-new UC Irvine campus, **the city emerged as an ideal fit for the expanding upper classes in Asia, especially fast-growing China**. Over the last decade, Chinese residents, the city's largest Asian group, made up about 10 percent to 13 percent of the population, before jumping last year to 17 percent.(Wheeler & Shimura, 2016 – emphasis added)

This city is growing and in my view it has a vetting process that includes the high median income and the sky-high rental rates. Few people can afford to live there unless they have the types of jobs that Irvine's corporate structure can offer. Not only that, but Irvine's plan is international in scope and it has its eye on Asia:

> High-income mainland China investment bankers, entrepreneurs, factory owners, actors and athletes began migrating to Irvine in larger

numbers about four years ago, said Zhihai Li, co-founder of WeIrvine, an internet-based service that helps Chinese immigrants settle in Irvine. Li said her 2-year-old service has 20,000 members and about 1,000 new members are signing up each month. Recent instability in China's economy has accelerated new millionaires' desire to invest overseas, at a time when Irvine is quickly adding houses on its way toward a projected population of about 328,000.(Wheeler, 2016)

Adding houses toward a projected population. That is where the developers come in. Irvine has the kinds of plans that rich cities tend to have: planning for parks and recreation, and as we will see, leisure activity:

The Orange County Great Park is taking shape, he said. The city in August hosted a grand opening of the first phase of the 194-acre Great Park Sports Park, which will be the biggest of its kind in Orange County — larger than Disneyland and Disney California Adventure combined. The Anaheim Ducks' community ice facility, the largest of its kind at least in California, is slated to open at the Great Park in November. (Shimura, 2018)

Competing with Disneyland. This place is a mecca. Not only that, but "an 18-hole golf course, a mile-long trail, a water park, a botanical garden, a permanent amphitheater, museums and a library are also planned at the Great Park. Wagner expressed support for a new aquatic center that could become the headquarters and a training facility for USA Water Polo. (Shimura, 2018) Here come the developers:

The city has also sued the county to stop its plan to develop 108 acres south of the Great Park into a **large, profitable residential and commercial complex.** (Shimura, 2018 – emphasis added)

These people are claiming to want to abandon growth, but they are really talking about "vetting" and keeping those racial and ethnic percentages under control, a kind of "financial sanitizing." According to one article,

One is an initiative, led by the group Irvine for Responsible Growth, that would give voters the power to weigh in on whether sizable development projects in the city can move forward. The group is collecting signatures to put the measure on a ballot. **Organizers said it's an effort to compete against lobbyists and campaign contributions from developers.**Wagner, however, said these residents want to "abandon growth." He said responsible growth helps **create affordable housing in the city and attract young talent.** (Shimura, 2018 – emphasis added)

Recall what I wrote elsewhere about the concept of "affordable housing"; whoever is in power reserves the right to define what is affordable and what is not. In a city like this, they are not talking about public housing, but providing housing for those corporate types who have the jobs.

> The second initiative, which will be on the June ballot, asks Irvine voters whether they support the City Council's approval of **a land swap with a developer that would put a state-run veterans cemetery on strawberry fields** near the I-5/I-405 interchange. A group of residents who want Irvine to stick to its original plan to donate city-owned property north of the Great Park for the cemetery collected enough signatures for the referendum. (Shimura, 2018 – emphasis added)

Strawberry fields forever. Large leisure parks, golf courses and cemeteries. The developers will have their hands full with these mega projects and the mayor will be right there to make sure he's "getting his cut."

Baltimore, (MD) Campaign and Power Broker Developers

Before we get into the money that was spent on a campaign that had more than 25 people in it, let me be the spoiler and let you know that a virtual underdog won the mayor's job. Here's some background:

> When Mayor Stephanie Rawlings-Blake announced in 2015 that she would not seek re-election this year, **a field of 29 candidates battled to lead Baltimore and tackle its many challenges**. There was a wealthy businessman who pledged to create jobs, a prominent Black Lives Matter activist who promised dramatic change and a disgraced former mayor looking for redemption. (Broadwater, 2016 – emphasis added)

Do you really think that the "challenges" were what these people all craved? Do you really think that a city steeped in racial division after that policeman shot down Freddie Gray was so attractive that twenty nine people would want to be the leader of it? Of course not. With that position, as we have seen in cities both larger and smaller than Baltimore, come the perks, the prestige and the power to work with "developers" to make mo' money, mo' money, mo' money!

Furthermore,

> Together, the leading Democratic candidates and several political action committees **pumped more than $9 million into the race** — triple the money spent on the last mayoral election in 2011. **State Sen. Catherine E. Pugh emerged as the victor of April's Democratic primary, the**

election that generally determines who will be mayor of deep-blue Baltimore. But Pugh had to withstand a spirited write-in challenge in November from former Mayor Sheila Dixon, a popular but controversial politician who left office after **being convicted of stealing gift cards.** (Broadwater, 2016)

Before moving on, let's take a comic break. You read it right – this sistah who was the leader of the city got busted – stealing gift cards. In a nutshell,

> She was the first African-American female to serve as president of the City Council, Baltimore's first female mayor, and Baltimore's third black mayor. On January 9, 2009, Dixon was indicted on twelve felony and misdemeanor counts, including perjury, theft, and misconduct. **The charges stem partly from incidents in which she allegedly misappropriated gift cards intended for the poor** … On December 1, 2009, the jury returned a "guilty" verdict on one misdemeanor count of fraudulent misappropriation and Dixon **received probation provided she resign as mayor as part of a plea agreement,** effective February 4, 2010. She was succeeded by the City Council president, Stephanie Rawlings-Blake, on February 4, 2010. (Wikipedia, 2018 – emphasis added)

This is reminiscent of when Texas congresswoman Eddie Bernice Johnson ripped off some scholarships, gave them to her relatives and then claims she didn't know the rules – rules that she wrote! (In August of 2010, Johnson violated organizational rules by awarding scholarship money to **four relatives of her own and two children of a top aide.** Awards come with **an anti-nepotism rule**, and winners must live or study in the Congress member's district. **Johnson said she "unknowingly" made a mistake in awarding the grants and would work with the foundation to rectify** it (Wikipedia, 2018 – emphasis added)

At any rate, the Dixon situation was reported on January 10, 2009, as follows:

> The case stems in part from at least $15,348 in gifts Dixon allegedly received from her former boyfriend, prominent city developer Ronald H. Lipscomb, while she was City Council president. She also is accused of using as much as $3,400 in gift cards, some donated to her office for distribution to "needy families," to purchase Best Buy electronics and other items for herself and her staff. (Linskey & Bykowicz, 2009)

Dixon ran a write-in candidacy and gave it a good try but Pugh ended up winning. And look at all the money that was spent to land the job:

> Warnock spent more than $2.7 million on the race, and **Pugh spent
> more than $2.5 million.** Dixon spent more than $1.2 million, while
> Embry spent $650,000; City Councilman Nick J. Mosby spent nearly
> $400,000, and City Councilman Carl Stokes and activist DeRay
> Mckesson each spent more than $300,000. (Broadwater, 2016 –
> emphasis added)

All that money to be mayor of the 26th largest city in America, with a population of 623,000. If they spent that much money competing for the job, can you imagine how much money is going to "change hands" behind closed doors once the developers and other shysters become involved?

But now let's back up to before the election and note a headline that carried the message, "Power Brokers Infuse Money into Baltimore Mayoral Campaigns." That was in January of 2016, a few months before the election and as you can see, that headline predicted exactly what would happen.

The article began, thusly:

> Who are the donors behind Baltimore's mayoral candidates? **Baltimore's
> power brokers** — some well known, some not — are once again
> placing their bets on who they want to become the city's next mayor.
> **Some are betting on everyone.** Donors with **ties to real estate
> developer David S. Cordish have given more than $60,000 to lawyer
> Elizabeth Embry's mayoral campaign.** Those with ties to **Baltimore's
> biggest demolisher of vacant buildings, contractor Pless B. Jones,
> have ponied up $17,000 for Sheila Dixon.** And, for a second time,
> Orioles owner Peter G. Angelos is backing Carl Stokes' bid for mayor.
> (Broadwater & Wenger, 2016 = emphasis added)

And the money just kept pouring in as the election crept closer and closer:

> **But lobbyist Frank Boston III, for instance, has donated to the
> campaigns of four mayoral candidates: Dixon, Stokes, state Sen.
> Catherine E. Pugh and City Councilman Nick J. Mosby.**
> Seawall Development Co. — which is developing heavily in Remington
> — has donated to Dixon, Stokes and businessman David L. Warnock.
> Ohio-based developers **The Woda Group have given to Pugh, Dixon,
> Mosby and Stokes.**"I like them all," Boston said. "They are my friends
> and, therefore, I support them. Each of the people that I gave to have
> faced critical deadlines in terms of fundraising, and I knew I wanted to
> help them toward their goal." (Broadwater & Wenger, 2016 – emphasis
> added)

And not one dime of this money is returnable or refundable. Free money – what white people call "welfare" when it's black people on the receiving end – for those who run for office, many of whom know they don't have a snowball's chance in hell of winning (like Jesse Jackson did when he ran for President in 1984, remember?). But Pugh won the election:

> **Pugh reported $664,000 available to spend — with about one-third of that ($222,000) coming from just 37 donors**. She received $12,000 from Daniel and Stephanie Hirschfeld of Genesis Rehab Services, $6,000 from Merrill Lynch and $6,000 from state Senate President Thomas V. Mike Miller. (Broadwater & Wenger, 2016)

She was connected because she had been a state senator before. She had her network and was ready to run for the position despite her lack of real name recognition.

> Francis X. Kelly, a former state senator from Baltimore County and a regent for the University System of Maryland, decided this election cycle to pick just one candidate for mayor to put his money on: Pugh. **He gave her the maximum $6,000."I just know how qualified she is. She is very reliable. She is very smart. She is understated,"** Kelly said. "When you need her and you make a call, she returns it." (Broadwater & Wenger, 2016 – emphasis added)

By being "understated" he means that she avoids controversy. No last names of previous black politicos, no stolen gift cards, no activist background. Just a woman who won a job as a state senator and sat on her ass and collected her paycheck.

Pugh won.

Minneapolis, (MN) Mayor's Race and Developer Contributions

Let's begin where we did in a few other cases: with the outcome of the election. After that, we go backwards and find out the REAL role that developer contributions played in getting the winner into the mayor's seat.

In an article headlined "Frey Wins Minneapolis Mayoral Race," the following was reported in November of 2017:

> Jacob Frey is the next mayor of Minneapolis. The Minneapolis City Council member emerged Wednesday **from a crowded field of contenders as the winner of Tuesday's election — a contest in which**

> **the city's ranked-choice voting system added to the drama.** Under
> ranked-choice, since none of the Minneapolis candidates won a majority
> of votes in the initial count Tuesday night, **election officials needed to
> continue moving through the ballots, counting voters' secondary
> choices until one candidate snagged a majority. It left city residents
> hanging about the final results.** (Frost, 2017 – emphasis added)

Remember that name because it will come back when we go back into the
pre-election contest and find out who got the money. At any rate,

> Frey had been leading in first-choice votes Tuesday night. By
> Wednesday afternoon, election officials said the tabulation of second-
> and third-choice results **showed Frey the winner, defeating incumbent
> Mayor Betsy Hodges, candidate Tom Hoch, state lawmaker
> Raymond Dehn and civil rights attorney Nekima Levy-Pounds.**
> (Frost, 2017 – emphasis added)

Now, the issue of housing and the role it played:

> **Frey put affordable housing among the key issues in his mayoral
> campaign, saying the city had lost 10,000 units of affordable housing
> in the last 15 years and needed a consistent solution.** He also called
> for the city's planning and regulation authorities to offer people **mixed
> and convenient land use and easy access** to the sharing and gig
> economy (Frost, 2017 – emphasis added)

And there you have it: the call for the city's planning and regulation
authorities is a summons to organize the developers and begin considering those
bids. And as we have seen with cities much larger than Minneapolis, this is when
the money begins to change hands.

And as for that gig economy, that has more to do with the types of workers
that will be hired. Simply, in a gig economy, temporary, flexible jobs are
commonplace and companies tend toward hiring independent contractors
and freelancers instead of full-time employees. In other words, more land and more
jobs with less pay.

With that having been shared in November 2017, we now go back before
Frey won the election, at a time when he was vying for the position and an article
from January headlines, "More Than $1.3 Pours Into Minneapolis Mayoral Race."

The article begins, thusly:

> **Three Minneapolis candidates have raised $200,000 or more in 2017,
> but deep coffers were not the deciding factor in the last mayoral
> election.** Minneapolis City Council member Jacob Frey, who is running
> for mayor, **leads the pack of candidates who released copies of their**

> **campaign finance reports, raising $359,879 this year**. Minneapolis has
> at least three big-money candidates running for mayor, according to
> campaign finance reports released Tuesday that showed more than $1.3
> million has already poured into the scramble for the top job at City Hall.
> (Belz, 2017 –emphasis added)

If deep coffers were not the deciding factor, then why did Frey win the election? Moreover,

> **Council Member Jacob Frey leads the pack of candidates who
> released copies of their reports, raising $359,879 this year.** He's
> followed by Tom Hoch, who raised $227,172 over the past seven months
> and loaned himself another $226,000. Mayor Betsy Hodges raised
> $204,138 and loaned her campaign $54,000. **It's a stark contrast from
> the last mayoral election,** when only two candidates — Hodges and
> Mark Andrew — raised more than $150,000 over the same time period.
> (Belz, 2017)

Of course there's a "stark contrast" from the previous election: Frey was ahead with more than #130,000 in contributions! He had his ducks in a row and the rich boys and fat cats came through for him. Frey was ahead and it stayed that way despite the following claim:

> But deep coffers have not been the deciding factor in recent mayoral
> elections, and the race for leadership of the state's largest city remains
> wide open because there is no primary to winnow candidates. Under the
> ranked-choice voting system, voters' second and third choices will also
> play key roles in determining the winner. (Belz, 2017)

Frey took the early lead and held it. And as we saw from the earlier article, he sewed it up in January. Again, his key positions were affordable housing and mixed and convenient land uses. Bring in the developers because this is when the money starts being applied for, considered and doled out..

Treasure Island, (CA.) Mayor's Race and Developers

This one is in a class of its down. We have two mayors who are linked by a slew of developers and as a group this contingent had a deal involving a lot of money. In the end the city actually handed over an entire area despite audits, voter anger and angry bureaucrats. Treasure Island is an artificial island in the San Francisco Bay and a neighborhood in the city and county of San Francisco. Treasure Island as a population of about 2,500.

In July 2010 an article by Allison Hawkes and Bernice Yeung appeared in the *San Francisco Public Press* under the headline, "Through Two Mayors, Connected Island Developers Cultivated Profitable Deal." Here is what took place. Let's walk through this.

> **In the next six months, local officials and a consortium of private developers will begin to finalize legal papers for Treasure Island's future as a high-density eco-city.** Renderings of the gleaming towers, parks and gardens suggest harmony and community. Yet the promise of an urban Treasure Island, one of the most complex and risky redevelopments in San Francisco's recent history, has for more than a decade been **wrapped up in a process driven by power and influence**. **The mayor got near total control.** Political friends **got plum jobs and contracts.** Critics were exiled. City and **state conflict-of-interest laws were waived.** Independent inquiries and the will of voters **were nakedly rebuffed**. (Hawkes & Yeung, 2010 – emphasis added)

What you just read is a prototypical example of a "conspiracy." The mayor and his coterie had it all figured out and dispensed control with extreme prejudice. These people all threw caution to the wind so that this "dream city" could be developed at a locale that is already an incredible tourist destination. It is about 34 miles from where I grew up.

Continuing:

> Big projects naturally draw big money. Treasure Island, currently slated for $6 billion in residential and commercial development, was an unusually large prize. **But companies with political and social ties to two mayors won the two major projects related to the redevelopment — with the master development drawing only one serious bid**. The winning bidder was a group that included Darius Anderson, an influential Democratic Party lobbyist and fundraiser for both **outgoing Mayor Willie Brown** and incoming Mayor Gavin Newsom. (Hawkes & Yeung, 2010)

Six billion dollars, but there were two mayors involved. Treasure Island's Mayor/Commission and the mayor of San Francisco. Willie Brown, the black man known for his expensive suits when he was a member of the California State Assembly, always had his hands in something. But this was the biggest prize of all even as he was stepping down. Who were the other "players" you may ask?

> One partner was the Miami-based homebuilder Lennar, **then the second-largest in the nation,** also now leading the concurrent $7 billion Hunters Point Shipyard redevelopment and the conversion of the former Mare

Island Shipyard in Vallejo. **Other companies, backed in part with public employee pension funds, have also joined the team now known as Treasure Island Community Development**. (Hawkes & Yeung, 2010 - emphasis added)

A mega sized development company from Miami, which is about 3,000 miles away. Another with a consortium of companies who wanted to pool together their monies so that they would be competitive.

At any rate,

> Over the years, few have been outwardly critical of the contracting process. An exception was former city supervisor and mayoral antagonist Tony Hall. During his brief tenure as head of the Treasure Island Development Authority he raised allegations — not all borne out by facts — **of missed deadlines, unpaid developer fees and a "sweetheart deal" in the making**. (Hawkes & Yeung, 2010 – emphasis added)

There it is! A "sweetheart deal." This was the first thing that I thought of when I saw the amount of money that was involved and the fact that there were two mayors involved. I knew that whoever had the most ties and networks was going to get the contract.

According to research,

> In 1998, **San Francisco voters attempted to wrest power from Brown and install good-governance practices for Treasure Island**. But supervisors never implemented many of the provisions in the ballot measure, which passed easily. Even today, some current and past city supervisors say they had to pick their battles, **and Treasure Island has been a remote concern**. (Hawkes & Yeung, 2010 – emphasis added)

Willie Brown was a hustler and knew his way around "making a deal". How many legislators do you know who are interviewed on "60 Minutes"? People from California know about Brown's reputation as a fast-talking money maker, described in Wikipedia (2018) as an American politician of the Democratic Party. Brown served over 30 years in the California State Assembly, spending 15 years as its speaker and later served as the 41st mayor of San Francisco, the first African American to do so. Under the current California term-limits law, no Speaker of the California State Assembly will be permitted to have a longer tenure than Brown's. Not only that, but The San Francisco Chronicle called Brown "one of San Francisco's most notable mayors" who had "celebrity beyond the city's boundaries (Gordon, 2004)

If Brown was involved in this Treasure Island deal, he need not have been present to be a player. His reputation was that he took care of his supporters and padded his administrations with various types of "aides." Put another way,

> Allegations of political patronage followed Brown from the State Legislature through his tenure as San Francisco mayor … **Brown is also criticized for favoritism to Ms. Carpeneti, the lobbyist with whom he had a child**. In 1998 Brown arranged for Carpeneti **to obtain a rent-free office in the city-owned Bill Graham Civic Auditorium**. Between then and 2003, a period that spans the birth of their daughter**, Carpeneti was paid an estimated $2.33 million by nonprofit groups and political committees controlled by then Mayor Brown and his friends** (Wikipedia, 2018 – emphasis added)

Friends. That's what it is called when people get favors from mayors. Not only that, but "Brown increased the city's special assistants payroll from US$15.6 to US$45.6 million between 1995 and 2001 … Between April 29, 2001 and May 3, 2001, *San Francisco Chronicle* reporters Lance Williams and Chuck Finnie released a five-part story concerning Brown and his relations with city contractors, lobbyists, and city appointments and hires he had made during his tenure as Mayor. The report concluded that there was an appearance of favoritism and conflicts of interest in the **awarding of city contracts and development deals …** (Wikipedia, 2018 – emphasis added)

And there you have it. The point I am making is that when Brown stepped down because of term limits, that didn't mean that his clout and connections were limited – the beat continued to go on with the Treasure Island project in my opinion. When Brown was in office he gave out city contracts to his pals. And "Brown put his former girlfriend, Wendy Linka, on the city payroll, as well as having appointed another former girlfriend and current U.S. Senator from California, Kamala Harris, to two California State boards in 1994 … (Wikipedia, 2018 – emphasis added).

Let me say that Kamala Harris may end up being President of the United States if her performances in the Senate, appearances on television and overall charisma and beauty are any indicator.

Keep that word "friends" in mind because,

> **Bill Rutland is a lobbyist and a close friend of Brown** who briefly worked on behalf of Anderson, the lobbyist, **to win the first part of the Treasure Island redevelopment bid.** He said that despite appearances, his team won the contract on merit. "Anybody that has the size and capacity to do these types of billion-dollar deals is going to have

relationships with the powers that be," Rutland said. "But they have to show a track record and a financial capability for doing that." (Hawkes & Yeung, 2010 – emphasis added)

And there's the link I was looking for. Brown may no longer be on the scene, but his "friends" most certain are. So now all we have to do is follow the money:

But Charles Marsteller, a former coordinator of San Francisco Common Cause, said no matter how dazzling the eco-city seems on paper, **insider politics represents a giveaway to companies with unusual access to government decision-makers.** "The public thinks we're going to build a city in the public's interest," he said. **"I would say we're building a city in the private sector's interest** — and whatever they want, we're getting. Ultimately the residents have to live with the **consequences long after the developer is gone."** (Hawkes & Yeung, 2010 – emphasis added)

And in this book I've shown this to be the case with smaller but very lucrative projects under the guise of "communities of interest," "planned communities" and newly developing suburbs. The key is that "insider politics represents a giveaway," and I don't care if it's Treasure Island, Hallandale Beach (FL.), Utah County or Lexington, Kentucky.

Willie Brown had this thumb in the pie from the get-go:

From the start, Treasure Island was Brown's pet project. In 1997, as the U.S. Navy began shuttering operations on the island, the former state Assembly speaker **parlayed his influence over the Legislature to push a bill establishing a separate governing authority for Treasure Island**. The move provoked opposition. A Brown political rival, former state senator and retired judge Quentin Kopp, suspecting Brown would appoint loyalists, fought against the bill. "He could control them," Kopp said. **"The objective was always to get the development power in the hands of friends and political supporters."** (Hawkes & Yeung, 2010 – emphasis added)

This was Brown's plan all along – a separate governing authority for Treasure Island, one that he would influence. The plan went on, as it was planned:

As expected, Brown won, and the articles of incorporation for the Treasure Island Development **Authority listed the San Francisco mayor as the "sole incorporator."** Directors would be named by the mayor "in order to perfect the organization of the Authority." City and state conflict of-interest laws forbidding city employees to hold dual offices were waived, **making it possible for Brown to pack the authority's board**. (Hawkes & Yeung, 2010 – emphasis added)

Brown was doing to white people and others what white people had been doing to the country and around the country for centuries. Like them, he surrounded himself with cronies and had his paperwork in order:

> **Former Planning Commissioner Gerald Green, one of Brown's original five appointees to the Treasure Island authority board, defended the entity's design** and said knowledgeable people like him belonged on it. "That was done not for mayoral control, but to have experienced people who could jumpstart the process," said Green, **who years later lost his planning job in an unrelated conflict-of interest scandal.** Also on the early board were the city's **directors of redevelopment and of the Port of San Francisco — both Brown campaign donors.** (Hawkes & Yeung, 2010 – emphasis added)

Experts in their field with experience, all on a board ready to do Brown's bidding. The staff was being built and the "waiver" ensured that there would be no outside interference:

> **Among the authority's staff were a number of "special assistants,"** a cadre of city employees hired by the mayor **without civil-service testing**. A 2001 civil grand jury report noted that some were scrutinized in the press as patronage jobs. The report named several Treasure Island staffers, including former director Annemarie Conroy. London Breed, **an unpaid intern in the mayor's office who was promoted to development specialist and secretary to the board**, now sits on the Redevelopment Commission. She defends Brown's integrity: "He was really aggressive **making sure the staff was by the book."** (Hawkes & Yeung, 2010 – emphasis added)

Brown had everything lined up and it was aptly named the Treasure Island Development Authority. According to the website, it is a "nonprofit public benefit agency dedicated to the economic development of former Naval Station Treasure Island. The Authority is vested with the rights to administer Tidelands Trust property. TIDA is also responsible for administering vital municipal services to Treasure and Yerba Buena Islands" (TIDA, 2018)

There is a seven-member Board of Directors which meets monthly on the second Wednesday of each month. The TIDA is staffed by the Office of the San Francisco City Administrator, with day to day operations and development planning led by Treasure Island Director Robert Beck. There is also a Citizen Advisory Board.

According to the article,

> With the Treasure Island Development Authority in place, **the city began priming the pump for redevelopment,** starting with modernization of the Clipper Cove marina between Yerba Buena and Treasure islands. Among the first bidders to surface was Treasure Island Enterprises, backed by star Democratic fundraiser Anderson and his former billionaire boss, Los Angeles supermarket magnate Ron Burkle. (Hawkes & Yeung, 2010 – emphasis added)

No sooner do these white men (or their negro imitators) get the paperwork done they make a mad dash for priming the pump for redevelopment. Bids for projects were submitted with the quickness, and Willie Brown remained the engineer:

> **Their ties with Brown ran deep. Both had been part of Brown's fundraising effort for his 1995 election campaign.** Burkle was a former law client of Brown's and donated to various Brown causes. The Anderson-Burkle bid immediately provoked claims that the outcome was a fait acompli, and a civil grand jury looked into it. The resulting 1998 report said the Clipper Cove marina's bidding process had never been made public "in an adequately informative way," **and called on the Treasure Island authority to use competitive, open bidding procedures**. (Hawkes & Yeung, 2010 – emphasis added)

But there was more in the report that Brown and his cronies had to pay close attention to:

> The report went on to decry **the lack of public oversight**, and said the process had been "hampered by concern about **the concentration of power, jurisdictional squabbling, political infighting."** In spite of these concerns, three bids came in and none was easy to dismiss. The Port of San Francisco reviewed the proposals, and each had its strengths and weaknesses. (Hawkes & Yeung, 2010)

The key words are "in spite of these concerns." These white men and their developer croneys don't "need no stinkin' badges"! They just do what they want and if there is a penalty or fine somewhere later down the road, they will be more than happy and prepared to pay it. The fact is,

> The plan had merit, but it didn't hurt **that Anderson and Burkle also had gotten to the right people.** Anderson told the San Francisco Chronicle that **he had paid lobbyist Bill Rutland, Brown's friend, $30,000** to learn "what were the hot buttons of the general public." (Hawkes & Yeung, 2010 – emphasis added)

There's always plenty of money spread around:

> **To develop the rest of the island, the Treasure Island authority issued a public call for a master developer in October 2000.** The brochure was sent out to 500 companies, and it boasted that the project was a "once-in-a-lifetime opportunity" **to redevelop the "jewel of the San Francisco Bay."** A few months later, the agency hosted a prebid conference and about 150 parties turned up. **But by the February 2001 deadline, only two bids had come in** … For example, the report said, the city could explain how it would assist with the redevelopment, and it could "make a selection based solely on qualifications."If adjustments were made, two developers said they would feel "very positive" about submitting a bid. (Hawkes & Yeung, 2010 – emphasis added)

A "master developer" meaning someone to put together a singular plan that would cover both commercial and residential development. There is no mention at all of "affordable housing" and that is because Treasure Island is going to be one of those "communities of interest" that apparently is aimed at general leisure and frolic.

On a website titled, "12 Things You Had No Idea You Could Do on Treasure Island," Brian Gerson offered the following snippets in his August 28, 2105 article. Treasure Island doesn't sound like much of a treasure unless you're a tourist, a wino or someone who wants to go fishing. The introductory snippet reads as follows:

> For most San Francisco residents, Treasure Island is good for one of two things: 1) the music festival, or 2) the flea market. Turns out though, there's way more to this tiny manmade island (that's only a seven-minute bus ride from SF!) than overrated EDM and cheap furniture. Here are 12 things you had no idea you could do on TI; just make sure you day-trip over there quick before someone turns it into one giant luxury apartment building.(Gerson, 2015)

As you look over the next dozen "things to do" you wonder why all the rancor and rigmarole and the billions in expenditures being proposed:

1. Brunch or lunch at Aracely,
2. Rent a beach cruiser at A Tran's bike shop
3. Definitely don't urban explore a bunch of terrifying irradiated houses
4. Try surprisingly good cocktails at Treasure Island Bar & Grill
5. Find out how the hell Treasure Island became Treasure Island
6. Try fresh-from-the-barrel wines at Fat Grape Winery

7. Test your bocce skills and drink wine in a submarine training vessel

8. Have a secluded picnic at Clipper Cove

9. Go paddle-boarding with Treasure Island Sailing Center

10. Check out a secret overlook

11. Visit Treasure Island's biggest winery

12. Fish from the most scenic fishing spot ever

All that money, planning, scamming and time invested and this is the best that San Francisco can come up with?

CONCLUSIONS

It is the developer who is key to the confusion and segregated state of the cities today. Mayors get all the publicity but in many instances – far more than stated in this book – the mayor and the local developers are in cahoots, working behind closed doors to rake in money.

Greed and profit are the motivating factors. And it is the mayor or the city leader who is seeking out a "legacy project" or two to make sure that once he's gone his name will live on forever. Assisted by various city administrations (I name as many as space would allow), these developers and other wealthy shot-callers are financing political campaigns, shifting the political focus of city planners and in all that, rarely residing in the areas of the city that they are intentionally manipulating.

This book has sought to analyze eighteen (18) cities and towns, areas that represent populations from the mega-large (New York, Los Angeles, Pittsburgh) to the ultra small (Palm Springs, Hallendale Beach, Lexington, Kentucky) and focus on the relationship between the mayors of those cities and the developers and what the relationships are like. I believe this book will be a necessary and sufficient starting point for understand how real "land use and politics" merge in these cities and why segregation by class and race continues to be the order of the day all over America.

You've seen the tendencies, the trends, the greed, the interlocking directorates and the way that city hall generates a handsome income for the mayor and those who, in the name of city planning, run shell game after shell game on a gullible tax-paying public. Additional research needs to be done because as long as the developer-mayor relationship exists, so will political graft, public chicanery and financial problems.

REFERENCES

Bagli, Charles V. (2013, December 15). Going Out With Building Boom, Mayor Pushes Billions in Projects. **New York Times**. Retrieved from https://www.nytimes.com/2013/12/16/nyregion/going-out-with-building-boom-mayor-pushes-billions-in-projects.html?mtrref=search.myway.com&gwh=3E9D08EF4ACAE953B05BC628CD7AB5DC&gwt=pay

Bandell, Brian (2018, April 25). Boca Raton Mayor Arrested for Allegedly Accepting Improper Funds From Developer. **South Florida Business Journal**. Retrieved from https://www.bizjournals.com/southflorida/news/2018/04/25/susan-haynie-arrested.html

Barkan, Ross (2016, May 17). De Blasio's Rivington Street Condo Debacle Is a Scandal That Just Might Stick. **Village Voice**. Retrieved from https://www.villagevoice.com/2016/05/17/de-blasios-rivington-street-condo-debacle-is-a-scandal-that-just-might-stick/

Bauder, Bob (2018, January 2). Pittsburgh Mayor Bill Peduto Wants to Focus on Development, Not Politics. **Trib Total Media**. Retrieved from https://triblive.com/politics/politicalheadlines/13136060-74/pittsburgh-mayor-bill-peduto-wants-to-focus-on-development-not-politics-in

Belz, Adam (2017, August 3). More than $1.3 Million Pours into Minneapolis Mayoral Race. **Minneapolis Star Tribune**. Retrieved from http://www.startribune.com/more-than-1-3-million-pours-into-minneapolis-mayoral-race/437982873/

Broadwater, Luke (2016, December 22). Catherine Pugh bested 28 other candidates to win Baltimore mayor's race. **Baltimore Sun**. Retrieved from http://www.baltimoresun.com/news/year-in-review-2016/bs-md-yir-mayoral-election-20161220-story.html

Broadwater, Luke & Wenger, Yvonne (2016, January 21). Power Brokers Infuse Money Into Baltimore Mayoral Campaign. **The Baltimore Sun**. Retrieved from http://www.baltimoresun.com/news/opinion/editorial/bs-md-ci-mayor-donors-20160121-story.html

Brooks, Ashley (2017, September 26). What is Urban Development? BizFluent. Retrieved from https://bizfluent.com/about-4728387-what-urban-development.html

Bryan, Susannah (2018, June 22) Hallandale mayor's arrest, commissioner's resignation set up November election. **South Florida Sun Sentinel**. Retrieved from http://www.sun-sentinel.com/local/broward/hallandale/fl-sb-election-hallandale-candidates-20180620-story.html

Bryan, Susannah & McMahon, Paula (2018, January 26). FBI Sting Leads to Hallandale Beach Mayor Joy Cooper's Arrest. **Fort Lauderdale Sun Sentinel**. Retrieved from http://www.sun-sentinel.com/local/broward/fl-sb-joy-cooper-arrested-hallandale-mayor-20180125-story.html

Christian, Paula & Lake, Hillary (2018, August 21). City of Cincinnati is owed $2.3M in overdue commercial loan payments from developers, citizens. WCPO – Channel 9. Retrieved from https://www.wcpo.com/news/insider/city-of-cincinnati-is-owed-23m-in-overdue-commercial-loan-payments-from-developers-citizens

City of Newark (2017, December 11). Mayor Baraka Creates Position to Ensure Residents Have Access to Affordable Housing Opportunities. Retrieved from https://www.newarknj.gov/news/mayor-baraka-creates-position-to-ensure-residents-have-access-to-affordable-housing-opportunities

Coolidge, Alexander (2017, November 13). Cincinnati Economy Fastest-Growign in the Midwest. **Cincinnati Enquirer**. Retrieved from https://www.cincinnati.com/story/money/2017/11/13/greater-cincinnatis-economy-fastest-growing-midwest/840139001/

Davidson, Lee (2018, July 13). Mia Love, Ben McAdams running neck and neck in money chase as Utah's hottest campaign gears up for stretch drive. **Salt Lake Tribune.** Retrieved from https://www.sltrib.com/news/politics/2018/07/13/mia-love-ben-mcadams/

Davis, Julie (2009) Urban catalysts in theory and practice. **Architectural Research Quarterly.** Retrieved from http://journals.cambridge.org/

Dulaney, Cody (2017, July 20. One Quarter of Fort Myers Mayor's Campaign War Chest Traces to 3 Developers. **Fort Myers News-Press**. Retrieved from https://www.news-press.com/story/news/2017/07/19/one-quarter-fort-myers-mayors-war-chest-traces-3-developers/493104001/

Eblen, Tom (2018, May 10). Mayor's Race Will Shape Lexington's Growth. Who is the Big Money Backing? **Lexington Herald-Leader**. Retrieved from https://www.kentucky.com/news/local/news-columns-blogs/tom-eblen/article210674584.html

Ehrenhalt, Alan (2016, November). The Reality of Mayors' Economic Promises. Governing the States and Localities. Retrieved from HTTP://WWW.GOVERNING.COM/COLUMNS/ASSESSMENTS/GOV-MAYORS-ECONOMIC-DEVELOPMENT-PROMISES.HTML

Erikson, a. (2012, August 24). A brief history of the birth of urban planning. **The Atlantic Cities.** Retrieved from https://www.citylab.com/life/2012/08/brief-history-birth-urban-planning/2365/

Flores, Cristina (2018, June 11). Salt Lake County Mayor to Host Meeting Over Controversial Olympia Hills Development. KUTV.com News. Retrieved from https://kutv.com/news/local/salt-lake-county-mayor-to-hold-meeting-over-controversial-olympia-hills-development

Frost, Evan (2017, November 8). Frey wins Minneapolis Mayoral Race. Minneapolis Public Radio Retrieved from https://www.mprnews.org/story/2017/11/08/minneapolis-mayoral-race-2017-final-result

Geissler, Jeff (2018, January 19). Bradbury Building Will Be Home to 16 New Apartments. **The Northside Chronicle**. Retrieved from https://www.thenorthsidechronicle.com/bradberry-gardens-set-to-open-in-march/

Gordon, Rachel (2004, January 4). The Mayor's Legacy – Will Brown 'Da Mayor' Soared During Tenure That Rivtals City's Most Notable, But Some Critical Goals Not met. **The San Francisco Chronicle.**

Grodach, Carl. (2008, June) Museums as Urban Catalysts: The Role of Urban Design in Flagship Cultural Development. **Journal of Urban Design**, 13, (2)

Halkias, Maria (2018, January 25) Black workers faced daily verbal abuse, including the N-word, at Plano construction site, lawsuit claims. **Dallas News**.

Retrieved from https://www.dallasnews.com/business/real-estate/2018/01/25/black-workers-faced-daily-verbal-abuse-including-n-word-plano-construction-site-lawsuit-claimshalkias

Hawkes, Alison & Yeung, Bernice (2010, July 1). Through Two Mayors, Connected Island Developers Cultivated Profitable Deal. **San Francisco Public Press.** Retrieved from https://sfpublicpress.org/news/2010-06/through-two-mayors-connected-island-developers-cultivated-profitable-deal

Kecseg, Ross (2017, April 21). Empower Texans.com. Plano Mayor Bankrolled by Special Interests, Raises Ethical Questions. Retrieved from https://empowertexans.com/metroplex/plano-mayor-bankrolled-special-interests-raises-ethical-questions/

Krause, Clifford (1997, August 22).)Arthur Ashe Stadium's Opening Serve Is in Giuliani's Court. **New York Times.**
Retrieved from https://www.nytimes.com/1997/08/22/nyregion/arthur-ashe-stadium-s-opening-serve-is-in-giuliani-s-court.html

Linskey, Annie & Bykowicz, Julie. (2009, January 10) Baltimore Mayor Dixon indicted. **The Baltimore Sun**. Retrieved from http://www.baltimoresun.com/news/maryland/politics/bal-md.ci.indict10jan10-story.html

Lord, Rich (2017, January 7). Calls Turn Developers into Donors for Peduto. **Pittsburgh Post-Gazette**. Retrieved from http://www.post-gazette.com/local/city/2017/01/08/Top-Pittsburgh-Mayor-Bill-Peduto-aide-s-calls-turned-developers-to-donors/stories/201701080036

McDonald, Jeff (2017, May 12). Mayor's Top Aide Got Married at Bayfront Estate of Developer and SoccerCity Supporter. **San Diego Union Tribune**. Retrieved from http://www.sandiegouniontribune.com/news/watchdog/sd-me-puetz-wedding-20170512-story.html

Millburg, Steve (2018) The 10 Best Harbors in America. **Coastal Living.** Retrieved from https://www.coastalliving.com/travel/top-10/best-harbors-usa

Musgrave, Beth & Ward, Karla (2018, May 22). Linda Gorton and Ronnie Bastin advance in Lexington mayoral race. **Lexington Herald-Leader**. Retrieved from https://www.kentucky.com/news/politics-government/election/article211665824.html

Nilsen, Ella (2018, May 22). Veteran Amy McGrath continues a Democratic winning streak for women and veterans. Vox.com. Retrieved from https://www.vox.com/2018/5/22/17381726/amy-mcgrath-jim-gray-kentucky-6th-congressional-district-women-veteran-2018-primary-midterms

Paybarah, Azi (2017, April 24). Dietl Questions de Blasio's Name and Heart. **Politico.** Retrieved from https://www.politico.com/states/new-york/city-hall/story/2017/04/24/dietl-questions-de-blasios-name-change-111468

Peiser, Ann B. & Peiser, Richard B. (2003). **Professional Real Estate Development: The ULI Guide to Business.** Washington, D.C. : Urban Land Institute.

Pilcher, James & Wert, Mark (2017, September 29). Biggest Donors to John Cranley, Yvette Simpson in Cincinnati Mayor Race? Developers. **Cincinnati Enquirer**. Retrieved from https://www.cincinnati.com/story/news/politics/elections/2017/09/28/biggest-donors-john-cranley-yvette-simpson-cincinnati-mayor-race-developers/704107001/

Real Estate Express (2018). Will a Felony Conviction Prevent Me From Getting a Real Estate License? Retrieved from https://www.realestateexpress.com/career-hub/become-a-real-estate-agent/will-a-felony-conviction-prevent-me-from-a-real-estate-license/

Reyes, Emily Alpert & Zahniser, David (2018, August 21). L.A. Ethics Comission tables proposed ban on developer donations. **Los Angeles Times**. Retrieved from http://www.latimes.com/local/lanow/la-me-ln-ethics-commission-20180821-story.html

Rice, Bradley R. (2018, September 1) Commission Form of City Government. Retrieved from http://www.tshaonline.org/handbook/online/articles/moc01.

Shatzman, Marci. (2018, April 27) Gov. Rick Scott suspends Boca Raton Mayor Susan Haynie. **South Florida Sun Sentinel**. Retrieved from http://www.sun-sentinel.com/local/palm-beach/boca-raton/fl-pn-boca-haynie-removed-04272018-story.html

Sheyner, Gennady (2017, January 20). After Re-Election, Palo Alto Vice Mayor Kniss Reaps Developers' Cash. **Palo Alto Weekly**. Retrieved from https://www.paloaltoonline.com/news/2017/01/20/after-re-election-kniss-reaps-developers-cash

Sheyner, Gennady (2017, October 5). New Housing Laws Pose Planning Challenges for City. **Palo Alto Weekly.** Retrieved from https://www.paloaltoonline.com/news/2017/10/05/new-housing-laws-pose-planning-challenges-for-palo-alto

Shimura, Tomoya. (2018, March 2). Here's What You Need to Know About Irvine Mayor's 2018 State of the City Address. **Orange County Register**. Retrieved from https://www.ocregister.com/2018/03/02/heres-what-you-need-to-know-about-irvine-mayors-2018-state-of-the-city-address/

Smith, Greg B. (2018, September 21). Controller Stringer questions city deal for expensive new DOI headquarters lease at heart of de Blasio dossier on Commissioner Peters. **New York Daily News**. Retrieved from http://www.nydailynews.com/new-york/ny-metro-controller-questions-doi-lease-20180921-story.html

University of Gronongen – Humanities Computing (1994-2012Retrieved from http://www.let.rug.nl/usa/outlines/government-1991/a-country-of-many-governments/city-government.php

Van Bueren, Ellen. (2018) Urban Development Management. Retrieved from https://www.tudelft.nl/bk/over-faculteit/afdelingen/management-in-the-built-environment/organisatie/leerstoelen/urban-development-management/

Wattenhofer, Jeff (2016, December 28). Mall Developer Rick Caruso and His Affiliates Have Donated $470K to City Hall. Retrieved from https://la.curbed.com/2016/12/28/14101552/political-donations-rick-caruso

Waxman, Andrea (2018, October 2). Panel Grapples with Gentrification and Low-Income Minorities. **Milwaukee Neighborhood News Service**. Retrieved from https://milwaukeenns.org/2018/10/02/panel-grapples-with-gentrification-and-low-income-minorities/?mc_cid=1873276756&mc_eid=98b2867f2f

Wetterich, Chris (2018, September 8). Former city manager said Cranley gave 'sweetheart deals' to developers, violated charter. **Cincinnati Business Courier**. https://www.bizjournals.com/cincinnati/news/2018/09/08/former-city-manager-said-cranley-gave-sweetheart.html

Wheeler, Ian & Shimura, Tomoya (2016, September 21) Why Asians have become the dominant group in Irvine – and what that means for the city. **Orange County Register**. Retrieved from https://www.ocregister.com/2016/09/21/why-asians-have-become-the-dominant-group-in-irvine-and-what-that-means-for-the-city/

Wigglesworth, Valerie (2017, May) Plano Mayor Harry LaRosiliere Wins Second Term Despite Large Vote for Anti-Apartment Slate. **Dallas News**. Retrieved from https://www.dallasnews.com/news/elections/2017/05/06/plano-mayors-race-may-headed-runoff-withanti-apartment-slate-attracting-voters

Winton, Richard (2017, February 16). Ex-Palm Springs mayor and 2 developers charged with corruption involving $375,000 in bribes. **Los Angeles Times**. Retrieved from http://www.latimes.com/local/california/la-me-ln-palm-springs-investigation-20170216-story.html

Woodson, Carter G. (1933) **The Mis-Education of the Negro**. Trenton, New Jersey: Africa World Press.